# TALES
*of a*
# MODERN
# SUFI

The Invisible Fence of Reality
and Other Stories

## NEVIT O. ERGIN

Foreword by Coleman Barks,
author of *The Essential Rumi*

Inner Traditions
Rochester, Vermont

Inner Traditions
One Park Street
Rochester, Vermont 05767
www.InnerTraditions.com

**Library of Congress Cataloging-in-Publication Data**

Ergin, Nevit Oguz, 1928–
  Tales of a modern Sufi : the invisible fence of reality and other stories /
Nevit O. Ergin ; foreword by Coleman Barks.
      p. cm.
  Includes bibliographical references and index.
  Summary: "A collection of modern Sufi tales by renowned Rumi translator
and Sufi initiate Nevit Ergin"—Provided by publisher.
  ISBN 978-1-59477-270-2 (pbk.)
  1. Sufi parables.  I. Title.
  PS3605.R48T35 2009
  297'.4—dc22

                                                                2008050141

Printed and bound in the United States by Lake Book Manufacturing

10  9  8  7  6  5  4  3  2  1

Text design and layout by Priscilla Baker
This book was typeset in Garamond Premier Pro with Calligraphic used as
a display typeface

To send correspondence to the author of this book, mail a first-class letter
to the author c/o Inner Traditions • Bear & Company, One Park Street,
Rochester, VT 05767, and we will forward the communication.

# TALES
*of a*
# MODERN
# SUFI

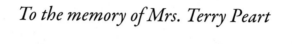

*To the memory of Mrs. Terry Peart*

# Contents

# The Unlearning

## Coleman Barks

NEVIT ERGIN AND I call each other *brother.* We have done that ever since we first met, whenever that was. It's hard to say because I feel as if I have always known him. We have shared many moments that feel as though they are outside of time: I have walked with him through the ruins of Yenikapi Mevlevihanesi, an old Mevlevi dervish community near Istanbul. We have sung hymns with Robert Bly in a fish restaurant on the Bosporus. And each of us has found a teacher.

How does one do that? It is one of the most mysterious of human processes, and perhaps unique for everyone. Reshad Feild has told his story of that in *The Last Barrier,* a very wonderful book. With regard to my own teacher, I met Bawa Muhaiyaddeen in a dream on May 2, 1977. I have described that meeting and the subsequent times with him on this more solid plane in several places, perhaps most succinctly in *Rumi: The Book of Love.* Nevit has told me a little about his meeting with his teacher, Hasan Shushud.

In 1956 Nevit had recently graduated from medical school and was conducting a residency in general surgery in Istanbul. For no reason that he consciously knows of, he was experimenting with various forms of fasting and holding the breath. The director of nursing at the hospital, an elderly gentleman, mentioned Hasan Shushud to Nevit and suggested that they go visit him.

The meeting did not happen right away. Nevit went into military service for two years and when he came back, the director had died. But a friend of Nevit's, a theater critic, told Nevit that his brother, a bank manager, wanted to see him. It turns out that before the head of nursing passed on, he had told this bank manager to find Nevit and take him to Mr. Shushud. They subsequently met at Hasan's house on the northern shore of the Bosporus.

Hasan asked Nevit why he was doing the breathing and fasting practices. Nevit said he did not know and that he had come to him to learn about such things. "This is not about learning, but unlearning," was Hasan's response. Nevertheless, Hasan gave him some pages that he had typed up. Nevit says he could not understand a word of them, but he did keep coming back to the house in Istanbul. He was shown techniques for observing the breath, but he still wanted *a book to read*. Hasan Shushud told him to get Rumi's *Divan,* as a book to help with the unlearning. And so began the adventure that has no end.

Rumi's great book, the *Divan-i-Kebir* (The Works of Shams of Tabriz), grew out of Rumi's annihilating friendship with Shams of Tabriz. Rumi died into that love. He became zero, and the poetry began to stream through the absence. This is what one learns from a teacher, how to dissolve the ego. It can happen through love, the heart opening that was their friendship. That *fana* (the denial of the self in the realization of God) becoming *baqa* (living with God) is what we feel in Nevit Ergin's massive twenty-two-volume translation of *The Shams*. Nevit translates from Golpinarli's Turkish translation of the original Persian. It is a tremendously generous act of devotion that he has given us.

Now Nevit comes with the gift of *these* stories, his own wholly original fables. You might say they are inquiries into the nature of human life, this astonishingly solitary consciousness that we endure, enjoy, suffer, inhabit. The stories feel honest and necessary, like pages torn from an explorer's notebook. The region being spoken of is not Antarctica, nor the high deserts of Central Asia, but rather whatever or wherever the word *spirit* points us toward. But not the afterlife—Nevit Ergin is interested in the here-and-now. His imagination takes us into the spirit dimension as it gets lived out in time, in place.

When I used to teach freshman English courses, I would try to find ways to reveal the ambiguous meanings of the stories my students were reading, the tableau scenes, the thematic images. But I would refuse, if asked, to teach *these* stories. They are not for school. They are for *unlearning*! For the mature human imagination.

There is a terrifying courage and loneliness in Nevit's world, all threaded through with a sense of fun. The sheer joy and play of creation is felt here. Nevit Ergin is a unique artist, and his lineage is unique too. Naqshband, Gurdjieff, Kafka, Beckett, Turkish folklore, Nasruddin, Rumi, and Shams of Tabriz, certainly.

A tiny black cricket hops onto the page that one of Nevit's first-person narrators is reading. He slams the book shut.

Now open this book, and watch what happens to *you*.

Coleman Barks, Ph.D., is an American poet who was born in 1937. In addition to publishing six collections of his own poetry, he is also a renowned translator of Rumi and other mystic poets of Persia, although he neither speaks nor reads Persian. (He bases his free-verse translations on other English translations.) Since 1976 he has published several volumes of Rumi's poetry, including *The Essential Rumi* (1995), *The Glance* (1999), and *The Book of Love* (2003). From 1967 to 1997 he was a professor at the University of Georgia at Athens, where he resides today. Through his translations of Rumi's work, Coleman Barks is widely credited with making Rumi, and in a larger sense Sufism, accessible to the English-speaking world.

# An Introduction to Sufi Teaching Tales

## Will Johnson

SUFIS ARE THE MYSTICS OF ISLAM, spiritual seekers whose long-ing and thirst cannot be satisfied by anything less than a direct personal experience of God. While the many different schools of Sufism have developed a multitude of different techniques designed to give the practitioner a direct experience of his or her intrinsic divine nature, common to all schools is their love of stories and storytelling as a way to express the most complex spiritual truths in simple and accessible language.

Sufi stories almost always present a common, everyday situation, but they inevitably present it with a twist that may leave you disturbed or, at least, thinking long after the storyteller has finished his or her account. Most of these stories were written long ago, though, and often reflect events or situations more reminiscent of times past than of the present day.

Enter Nevit Ergin. Nevit is a round and gentle, unassuming, and exceedingly humble fellow who has spent the better part of his eighty years on this planet under the spell of Jallaladin Rumi, the great thirteenth-century poet, mystic, and developer of the dance of the whirling dervish. Nevit became enamored with Rumi's extraordinary words and language as a young man and decided to commit himself to translating all of Rumi's poetry into English for a new culture and generation to enjoy and be inspired by. Most of his friends and colleagues told him he was crazy to attempt this as Rumi's writings comprise forty-four thousand verses that were collated over the years into twenty-three volumes! Nevit is also very tenacious, though, and he has managed to complete his life's work. In fact, many of the "translations" of Rumi that you may know and love are not technically translations but are rather edited reworkings and rewordings of Nevit's original translations from Turkish into English. If the explosion of interest in Rumi's writings can be traced to any one door, Nevit's is the most likely candidate.

Even less well known is the fact that Nevit is a lover of the tradition of Sufi stories, and while he was busily translating Rumi's poems, he also found time to compose Sufi stories of his own—and what stories these are! Nevit's world is one in which the ordinary and the extraordinary collide and interact and in which it is often difficult to differentiate between the two. They are also often harrowingly poignant. Some of them read like mystical dreams, others like everyday nightmares. Nevit's is a world of penny arcades and pawnshops, of fishing boats and circuses. He knows all about the everyday crises of financial worries and marital troubles. And he knows that the only way to figure out the life that we are living is to come to terms with the death that awaits us. As the Sufi says, "Die before you die." What can that possibly mean?!

As simple as his stories may appear to be, they have a mischievous way of getting under your skin, far under, way deep down into areas of your psyche that you ordinarily rarely access. They may start with the simplest kinds of observations only to veer off into unknown territory that may leave you with feelings and responses that you may have a hard time recognizing. You may start a story thinking that you're taking a simple drive to the corner store only to realize that it would have been better if you had fastened your seat belt and shoulder harness and maybe even put on a crash helmet!

So dive in to these stories the way you slip in to a bath, but be prepared that there may be some things lurking at the bottom of the tub that you didn't realize were there. And above all, enjoy the simple language and voice of a master wordsmith whose only intention is to shake you up and help you come out of your slumber.

◆

Will Johnson is the founder and director of the Institute for Embodiment Training, which combines Western somatic psychotherapy with Eastern meditation practices. He is the author of several books on Rumi, including the award-winning *The Spiritual Practices of Rumi* and (with Nevit O. Ergin) *The Rubais of Rumi* and *The Forbidden Rumi*. He is also the author of *The Sailfish and the Sacred Mountain* and *Yoga of the Mahamudra*.

# TALES
*of a*
# MODERN
# SUFI

# Preface

IN 1957 I MET A REMARKABLE MAN. His name was Hasan Shushud, and he was then in his late fifties. He told me, "Son, keep fasting; breathe the way I show you. When the time comes, with a little bit of suffering, you'll get there."

I asked, "How about books, and teachers?" He suggested I read Rumi's *Divan*. As for teachers: "You are your own." I then asked about the "do's and don'ts," to which he listed: "Be like everybody else, there is no dress code, marry and earn your living, don't be a burden to others." Then he added, "This is a long, lonely journey, and the road is paved with fire. But it is the only way." Gradually, slowly—like the emerging seasons—changes took place in me over a long period of time, irrespective of a particular date or event.

I have pursued a busy, intense professional life. At home I shared the suffering of someone who lived the hell of schizophrenia.

I fasted for close to twelve years; I translated Rumi's *Divan*, and I wrote these stories. They are based on a different perception of time and space where reality becomes possibility, creation is a potentiality, and life a hallucination. Self becomes a hair in the eye, a thorn in the bottom of the foot. Like wearing tight shoes, being fully present in the moment—each and every moment—constantly hurts consciousness.

Many attempts have been made to escape from this dungeon

3

of existence without a proper realization that the key is in the hand of the prisoner.

In these stories, humanity is described as the children of perception, not Adam and Eve. Man is a concept rather than an object. Like a shore or horizon, he fluctuates between the known and unknown. Here, immortality becomes the destiny of human-kind. Since one has never been born, one never dies.

Eternity is the backyard of the one who annihilates the self. Without this process no one can see beyond the cosmic illusion—this magnificent lie—and one remains like a bird without wings, dormant and prone on the ground.

The issue of death is the center of all these stories. (How could it be anything else when death remains the absolute mystery?) Man's organic existence is so short and fragile that every belief system offers some sort of permanency as a consolation. These sys-tems utilize very earthly terms; when the body lays in the grave, the soul experiences all kinds of pleasures and pains, depending on if the person was a believer or unbeliever. One who does not register with this belief accepts that life was a party with death as the end. For others, death is somebody else's affair.

In these stories there is neither an intellectual or moral persua-sion, nor the discussion of faith and reason. Instead, excitement, freedom, liberation, and ecstasy are mentioned. Since man's behav-ior is the shadow of his Essence, all attempts to change the direction of the shadow are considered illusionary. Instead one should try to change the Essence through one's eating and breathing habits, while experiencing contrition; living the full extent of every day's life is the best way to experience the suffering necessary to burn the fire.

One must also recall that the world is only a thrift store—full of mere bits and pieces—and not a place to search for silk carpets.

# Any Suggestions?

I HAVE BEEN SITTING on this rock for so many days and nights, listening to the sound of the waves.

One of my feet is in the sea, the other on the sand. I have watched so many sunsets and sunrises. I saw stars and all kinds of moons. Airplanes have passed over me. I have seen ships filled half with sorrow, still others with hope.

How did I get here?

One day I decided to leave the city. I drove my car as far as I could. I knew when a man lives on an island, if he goes far enough he'll end up at the sea. I left the car where the road came to an end. I walked and walked until I could hear and smell the sea.

Sure enough, the sea was there with all of its beauty and might. I took a long leisurely walk on its deserted beach. I met a few dogs here and there. Then, I noticed this rock. I settled there. It was the ideal spot to concentrate on God. This was what I was going to do. My decision was either to find Him or die. Anything between was not worth living for anyway.

Searching for Him in the city—among people, books, and temples—frustrated me. The only thing left for me was to go into isolation and concentrate on Him.

My staying at the same spot caused some curiosity. A black dog came from nowhere. First, he kept a distance from me, but gradually he came closer. He was cautious and tried to get my scent. Then he became my friend. He wanted to become my dog. I said, "Why do I need a dog here while trying to unload myself?" I believe the dog sensed that, and gradually he backed off and disappeared.

After that, a rider stopped his horse, which, like the dog, was black. He asked me, "What are you doing there?" He said that all this land belonged to him.

Instead of arguing, I answered, "My dear man, I am not occupying your land. Look, only one foot is on your land, the other is in the sea. I am on the shore and don't belong to the sea or the land. Besides, if you allow me to stay here, my friends will come to visit me. You can charge them a fee."

Liking my idea, he wished me luck and left.

One morning, after a nightmare the previous night, I woke up and found a body in front of me on the shore. The corpse was mine. It was my own body lying there. I was scared. Nevertheless, I went and examined it carefully. It had everything, all the marks and scars I have carried for years. Giving up to the earth this body I had carried like my own all these years made me sad. I knew the body wouldn't last long there. The birds and fish were already gathering.

I felt an obligation to discard it with some dignity. The first thing that came to my mind was throwing it into the sea. It would be easy since the sea was next to me. I carried the corpse to the edge of the cliff and threw it as far as I could. The body came back to the shore, next to me, the following morning. The sea expels everything that doesn't belong to it.

Next, I tried to carry it as far as I could. I dug a big hole, buried the corpse there, and put a big stone on top of it. I was happy. I felt good. I returned to my place. As long as this leftover was out of my sight, I could continue my life.

I found the corpse the next morning where I had been sleeping. I carried it back again and buried it even deeper. But the same thing happened the following nights. I was shocked, scared, and frustrated. Later, I realized I was the one who had removed my own body from the grave during my sleep and laid it next to me.

Then it occurred to me that I could use the wind to get rid of this unnecessary, functionless item that was no help in my life. I transported the body to the top of the rock where the wind blew the hardest and left it there for the wind to do the rest. But it was at the top of another rock the following day. While I was preoccupied with this unholy business, I almost forgot my initial, noble mission: to find God.

One evening I saw a faint light flashing from the top of the mountain just behind me. I waited till morning to explore it. There was an old building there I hadn't noticed before. It was an old lighthouse built of stone. It had a small door and a few small windows. The following night, I confirmed the flashing light was coming from it. I even felt as though someone was sending me a message.

It was really hard to climb the mountain with the weight of my body on my shoulders. I had no other choice but to find out what was up there. The water, earth, and wind had denied my effort in getting rid of my own corpse.

The building stood alone. There was no other sign of life around. I knew there were people inside. It was the first time I was happily expecting to see a human. I left the body outside the door then climbed the stone stairway and found two men in front of the upstairs fireplace. One was short, fat, and bald. The other was tall and skinny with a pipe in his mouth. Both were dressed in old-fashioned leather pants with red shirts, and their chests were bare. Neither of us was surprised to see each other. I greeted them and asked, "How long have you been here?"

They said they had forgotten. The last visitor before me was a guy named Ovidus. He had come to stay with them after he was kicked out of Rome. I was sure that had happened fifty some odd years before Christ was born.

It was apparent that we somehow knew each other. They helped me to carry my corpse to the stairs. I felt comfortable enough to tell my story, so I explained my problem. "I am frustrated," I said. "I am trying to find God, but this old body of mine keeps getting in my way and stopping me. How can I get rid of it?" I continued to explain my adventure. "I dumped it in the sea, but the sea didn't accept it. I buried it in the sand, but it was I this time who removed it every night in my sleep. The wind wasn't helpful either."

The small, fat one said with a toothless smile, "Your trouble is over."

I was not convinced. "You are a couple of weird guys left over from history. Even your own people have forgotten you! How old are you anyway?" I asked.

They looked at each other, "We don't know," they answered. "Time has stopped for us."

The fire was burning in front of us in the fireplace. The short one repeated, "Your problem is over." Looking into the fire, he said, "We can help you."

I thought he was right; water, air, earth . . . only fire is left. After all, fire is probably the best purifier.

We threw the corpse in the fire. I closed my eyes. I didn't want to see burning flesh. When I opened my eyes, I wanted to see ashes. But alas, the body was still there, unchanged, resisting the burning appetite of the flames. I was as horrified as the others. The fire burned itself out, but the body remained.

After a few more attempts we all gave up. They loaded my body on my shoulders again. As I was leaving, one of them made this short remark: "Maybe this is your ticket to Heaven," he said. Then he added, "Either it will bury you or get you there."

So I returned to where I had begun: to the town, the people, my job, and home. But I am still looking for a way out of this.

Any suggestions?

# No Wall Around

THREE OF US FROM THE SAME WARD decided to run away from the mental hospital. We didn't think we belonged there, even a doctor said so. He's not a doctor anymore though; he became one of us. Anyway, we were tired of listening to the same old stories about the real world from the elderly. We wanted to find it for ourselves.

Before we attempted to escape, we sent Smarty (the wisest insane among us) to explore the field around and check out the wall that has kept us prisoners all our lives. Smarty came back a couple of days later, exhausted, hungry, and mostly disappointed.

"Friends, we cannot escape. There is no wall around," he explained.

After a silence I said, "We'll make one and then jump over."

Smarty answered, "It's no use, we are prisoners of our own perception, not the wall."

"Then," I said, "we will change our perception."

"That is not easy," he answered. "Look at Joe. He doesn't eat, doesn't talk. But he's still here, not there."

Since Joe decided not to talk, he carried a small blackboard, hanging around his neck. When he wanted to say something, he would write it on his board.

"Smarty," he wrote. "What is here, what is there?"

# The Unemployed Shaman

*SINCE LIFE WILL DROP ME ONE DAY, why shouldn't I drop life first?*
I thought.

I had lived most of my time in and out of the invisible fence of reality, shifting endlessly between fact and fantasy. I hoped one day to find a way out of this three-dimensional perception.

I had been told that the polar twilight would wash away the necessity for belief or disbelief, that the northern lights would create a new organism out of my tired, aged body.

I journeyed to the north the way whales, birds, and all other creatures are drawn to their destination.

A small, two-seater charter plane left me at an Eskimo village one afternoon with the promise to return before winter set in. The small village turned out to be a ghost town, except for a few old, sick natives.

There were some people who had been left to save the whales squeezed between the icebergs; others were picked up by spirits from the sky.

The one who was in charge of maintaining the bare necessities for the old and sick was a middle-aged man who called himself Shaman.

"You must explain to me what this thing is called life," I said.

He smiled. "Fish would know the water if they discovered the air."

I was hoping to hear more than that, but that was all I could get from him. There were no books, icons, temples, or lecture halls around.

I had settled down to a routine of the simplest chores in life: fishing, gathering a few plants, caring for the elderly and the sick.

I listened to the frozen silence during the days that got shorter and shorter in this Province of the Lost. At night I sat down with Shaman in front of the fire. He kept chanting all night long. Eventually, I joined him. It sounded like an endlessly prolonged song; my body as well as my soul contracted and expanded to its epileptic rhythm. I wished I could cry but was unable to because I was not innocent enough.

One morning he woke me up. It was the first time I had seen him excited.

"They are coming," he said.

"Who?"

"Spirits. You will meet them."

I looked at his face, wondering if I was ready.

"Yes, you are, and keep busy brewing herbs and packing backpacks with blankets and sleeping bags."

We took off that afternoon to head toward the hills. He was walking briskly ahead of me, and I had a hard time keeping up with him. I asked if he would slow down.

He pointed to a cliff and said we had to reach it before dark.

I was afraid to ask what was up there. When we finished climbing, we were at a small cave carved in the ice. There was some left-over food on the floor. Apparently, he came here frequently. He put the blankets, thermos, and food package in one corner.

"You will wait for the spirits here," he said.

I looked at his face, begging for help. "Alone?"

"Alone. I will return to the town."

I was afraid. He knew that.

"There is a time for everyone to find out what's up there," he said as he pointed to the sky. "This is your time."

He left silently, leaving everything behind. Night soon lit all the stars. I became like a small frozen insect at the center of the thick, icy silence. I lay down in the sleeping bag, my eyes open, my body cold and still. I reached for the thermos. There was hot tea that Shaman had brewed from plants he had carefully collected.

I swallowed a couple of sips of tea. It tasted bitter and spicy, and I drank more. A few hungry wolves were crying outside. I waited and waited, then fell asleep.

When I woke up, the sky was burning a dark red. I went outside. I saw a cold green covering part of the red. Something majestic was happening. The most unusual colors were flowing across the sky from north to south with the rhythm of a divine symphony. I was totally overwhelmed by the challenge of the colors and sounds trying to outdo each other. I knew I was witnessing a miracle.

When I turned back from the sky, I saw my body lying down in the cave, inside the sleeping bag, like a silkworm buried inside a cocoon. I lost all sense of time and place. I understood now what Shaman had said about the fish.

Maybe this divine show in the sky was nothing but a natural phenomenon called the Aurora Borealis, or maybe I was hallucinating from the drink that Shaman had brewed. It didn't matter. I knew I wasn't the one buried in the cocoon; I was outside where there were lights and colors and sounds that could be seen and heard by all who would perceive them.

When I came down to the village the next day, Shaman didn't

say a word. I asked a few old folks if they had seen the Aurora last night. They shook their heads. One old man told me the last one had appeared many years ago and had taken some of the townspeople to the sky. I felt like I was one of those who had been taken.

"I want to go back to the place I came from and help people," I said to Shaman.

"Stay here. The thirsty come to the fountain. The fountain doesn't go to them."

"But I need to be needed."

"There is not much use for a shaman where you come from. You will be sorry."

I didn't listen to him.

I filled out many applications and knocked on many doors after I came back. No one answered me. Times were very hard for an unemployed shaman.

# The Purpose of
# Creation Is
# Perception

MY FORTUNE HADN'T BEEN the best lately. My wife had left me, taking the children and everything else. I was out of work, my dog had disappeared, and winter came unexpectedly early.

This could have been the bottom for me or things might still become infinitely worse. I was scared and at the same time excited.

All the failures, defeats, humiliations, and losses had made me content rather than depressed. I had no religion, no desire for life, and no hope for heaven.

My question was an old one, as old as the universe. It was about life and death. How could there be anything else without the answer for that? All other questions were absurd and trivial. In all the years of my life, I hadn't come close to the answer, nor had I ever seen anyone else who had.

It would be naive of anyone who examined this writing to expect to find the answer at the end. All I could ask was that my writing be read and then reread.

I wanted to make me die so that I could step out of my body

and look at the beyond. As Camus said: "There always comes a time when one must choose between contemplation and action. Man is his own end, his only end."

Among the few options available to achieve that end, I chose fasting because it was simple, inexpensive, and less messy. The difference between hunger and fasting was a matter of choice.

I skipped breakfast and lunch. I didn't drink or smoke. Hunger was a mild pain at first, then grew as a dark shadow. After that night and the next morning, a calm settled in.

On the third day of fasting, I wasn't hungry at all. I felt light-headed, had a dreamlike perception of the world around me, and my breathing had changed.

It was late afternoon when I sat on the floor. The only thing left in the room was the picture on the wall. It was a very inexpensive, rather confusing, busy oil painting by some unknown artist. I had bought it from a Salvation Army store. Nobody had bothered to take it; it was worth nothing.

I sat in front of it and noticed for the first time that a series of landscapes were overpainted on the same canvas.

Once I started separating the layers of pigment, I discovered mountains full of snow with pine trees. Beneath the alpine scene was a river with all kinds of bridges. Under that was a pond with water lilies. At the bottom was a seascape.

The sun was shining over a calm sea. The rays of the sun were melted with gold on a series of hills on the left side. They were also on fire with the sun. A narrow path extended along the shoreline.

The time could have been sunset or sunrise, but this painting was all about the moment in which everything looked the same, regardless of which direction the sun would go.

This was a totally new perspective where the past, present, and future merged. It wasn't an abstract feeling. I experienced this undivided time as an intense ecstasy. I felt the warmth of the sand on my feet and the heat of the sun through my eyelids. I heard the sound of waves. I smelled the sea.

"Is it possible I could be there while I am still here?" I could not answer my own question.

My feelings gradually became more intense. Someone called my name, and I opened my eyes.

I was definitely there sitting on the sand. I heard the sea gulls and saw a fisherman pulling nets from the ocean. He was the one calling me. I felt too weak to get up and help him, but he kept summoning me. He was up to his knees in the water.

Later I found I was standing next to him, holding the net. We started pulling on it. At the end of the net was my body, looking like an old dead fish. When I touched it, it disintegrated into fibers and disappeared. So did the fisherman and sea gulls. I was standing at the shore alone.

The waves were breaking into white foam right at my feet. I saw a woman with children walking along the shore. They were poorly dressed. She had on strange makeup. Her lips were like a knife wound. Her eyes were cold and distant. They gave me no recognition and walked away.

I saw other people. They came from nowhere, and they went to nowhere.

After all my images faded away, creation ceased to exist, and the rapid succession of the scenes on my perception stopped. I felt bare, without memories, without dreams.

I saw the fisherman once again. He asked me if I was scared.

"Yes," I said. "Living was something I was used to, even in my misery. I had hope there, hoping to get out. Now I am out of everything, without myself."

"No. No," he said. "You are still with yourself. You are right here." He was pointing at the shoreline. "You are between the known and the unknown, between earth and heaven."

I wanted to touch the shore. I touched the sand, then the water, but not the shore.

"The shore is a concept," he said, "not an object. So is man."

I was worried. "Am I going to live like that?"

"Living? Don't you see you are not even breathing?"

I was without breath. I felt chills all over me. Then I became aware that he was reassuring me, trying to calm me down.

"For each breath, creation repeats itself from nothing to everything and back to nothing. This happens so fast the ordinary mind doesn't register the action. You have a taste of timelessness. Traveling in time is nothing but exploring the layers of perception."

"Who are you?" I asked. "What do you want from me?" He did not give me an answer, but asked a question instead.

"What do you want from me?"

"I want to know more, so I can change my life, my reality," I told him.

"The more you know, the less you try to change life. Reality is not real."

I was back in my room, sitting on the floor in front of the painting. The sun was still on the horizon. The sea was calm, and my footprints were on the sand.

"What am I doing here?" I decided I simply lived here.

# The Next Harbor

A SMALL, BLACK SAILBOAT brought me here and left me at the harbor.

Like at the beginning or end of a strange story, I felt tense and uneasy. I watched the sunset until the last shaft of light was gone.

I slept with mermaids and listened to the surf all night. Then the sun came above the horizon to turn the highways along the shore to gold.

I saw people, singly and in groups, dressed in white garments that came up on one shoulder. Some were bare-chested. All of them were walking in the same direction.

I wanted to walk the other way, but I couldn't face them and greet them at the same time, so I walked behind them.

It was a long, slow journey.

I saw the sea grapes, half-full, half-empty, among the drying mosses scattered about the shore.

I saw live and dead fish, colorful shells, and sea horses.

We arrived at a hotel of white marble built on the hill with stairs and terraces coming down to the beach.

Everyone was climbing the stairs silently, so I did the same.

I occasionally stopped to look back. The view got better and better as I climbed higher.

This wasn't the horizon, and this wasn't the sea. What I

saw had all the kindness of a mother caring for and nursing my imagination.

In the distance were ancient ships getting fresh water from an aqueduct built over the columns at the small offshore island. An old castle marked the beginning of the spice road.

When I was totally exhausted, I stopped at that level and walked into a hallway that ended at a door. I had no key, nor did I know the secret word, but the door opened by itself into a large room.

There were a few tall, black eunuchs conversing with each other in mellow, sweet voices, and several dwarfs were entertaining the guests. Nobody noticed my existence. I seated myself on one of the pillows on the floor. I sensed we were all waiting there for the arrival of someone very special.

Time went by. The shadows got longer, and the room got darker. The management made excuses for the power failure and lit candles.

I watched my candle as it burned slowly but surely down to the nub, and the entertainment went out. The guests, eunuchs, and dwarfs had disappeared somewhere. I wanted to get out, but found the doors and windows were all locked.

That special someone I had anticipated all this time was Night. It was starless and dreamless. I didn't need my eyes and other senses to see that.

I let myself go. I plunged into darkness.


I expected the small boat with the black sails to take me away again and carry me across an ocean where eternity was nothing but one small wave.

I did not know where or when or at which harbor this story would end, or start again with different sunrises.

# County Fairs

I LIKE COUNTY FAIRS, especially in the evening when the air smelled of dust, beer, barbecue, people, and with the lights flashing all over and the music screaming.

There were men in their big white hats and boots, women wearing jeans with flannel shirts, and kids with fanny patches roaming around.

Summer was usually over by the time the fair came, but its final lingering breath haunted me with the touch of fall and coolness in the air.

The lighted trees looked divine, and the booths and tents were filled with dirt and noise under the big branches.

I sat on the grass in front of the merry-go-round for hours. I would also walk around the roller coasters, bumper cars, and super slides, trying to share the joy and exuberance I saw on the faces of the children. Teenage boys and girls walked hand in hand, stopping occasionally to throw darts at balloons. When they hit the target, I felt I had won all those blue and pink stuffed animals.

At the very edge of the fair there was always a big tent, open all around. Inside were bleachers set in a half-moon.

When I was tired, I would sit there and wait for the next show.

One night I got there quite late. The last show had been over for almost an hour. There was no one at the circus. All the lights were off except for the one on the stage. I sat in the middle of a front bench drinking a cup of coffee. The fair was still going on in the background.

Suddenly, a little boy, maybe eight, walked to the center of the stage. He had no shirt, no shoes. His hair was long, his face was dirty, but he had a distinct smile that deepened a small dimple on his left cheek.

First, he bowed to a nonexistent audience. I knew he couldn't see me. Then he raised his hand and ordered an unseen musician to start. A cheerful carnival music filled the air. Then he started to dance with a frantic rhythm, whirling, kneeling, jumping. His feet were bare. He went on and on with great joy, yelling and screaming. Then he stopped, bowed again, and ran off the stage.

I applauded and ran after him. There were mobile homes and campers behind the circus tent. He disappeared among them.

I thought he must be the son of one of the performers. I very much wanted to talk to him, but I was tired and knew how hard it would be to find him.

I slowly returned to the fair and noticed the crowd had thinned. There were still a few lines of children waiting to get in the magic house, and some people were still eating and drinking at the food stands.

I was slowly walking toward the exit door when I saw the boy again. He was walking ten yards ahead of me. He was alone, and there were people between us. I quickened my pace to get closer to him. He also started walking faster, and then started running. I ran after him but lost him in the crowd.

I got to the gate and waited to see him. I even asked the officer if they had seen a young boy with bare feet. Nobody knew anything about him.

I knew the night was not over for me. I couldn't leave the carnival. I turned back and walked toward the midway. I was the only one going in that direction. I passed the rides, the magic houses, and the booths until I once again reached the empty circus tent.

My coffee cup was still on the bleachers where I had left it. The stage light was on, and absolutely nobody was in the tent.

I sat in my old place. The coffee was cold and tasted bitter. I had a funny feeling. I knew he was around and following me.

I was right. He came running to the stage again, without shirt or shoes. He had a dirty face and a sweet smile. I stoop up and applauded.

He bowed to me, then to the audience. He turned to the musicians, raised his hand, and started the music. He danced, whirling, clapping his hands, and tapping his feet.

"Bravo," I yelled. "Bravo!"

He raised his hand to thank me. He stopped and stood on the stage. I walked toward him.

"You are the best dancer I have ever seen."

He smiled.

"Who are you?" I asked.

"I dance differently every night," he said.

"What's your name? Where are your parents?"

He smiled. "Now it's time for me to go down the super slide once more."

I realized he lived in a different world and was not about to get involved in mine. I tried very hard to have a conversation with him, but he did not bother to answer me.

We had a two-track conversation. He kept telling me all about the rides and games at the fair. I kept asking all the wrong questions about his life: who he was, where he came from, and who he belonged to. In the end I was tired and frustrated. I asked him if he wanted a drink, and he said he did. I went to the closest food stand to get him one.

When I came back he was gone. I very well knew the futility of running around looking for him. I sat on the bleachers helplessly.

I saw a small wallet next to me, then immediately recognized that it was my first wallet, given to me on my eighth birthday. My picture was inside. I saw a small, eight-year-old boy with long hair, a sweet smile, and a dimple on the left cheek.

I remembered this boy. I knew I had lost him forever at the county fair.

# Just Like
# Anybody Else

I TRAVELED THIS ROAD every day on my way to work in the morning and again at night on my way back home. It took me through the poorest section in town. Here were the low-income families: oil workers with tattooed arms, new mothers pushing strollers on the narrow sidewalks. There were a few restaurants, a laundromat, and a couple of gas stations. Sometimes under the blazing summer sun the asphalt of the sidewalk melted, making the air smell of oil. The people were old, fat, or pregnant. Life in this place was ugly.

At a corner, on the back of a lot, was an old junk store. The yard in front of the store was overcrowded with old iron beds, a few dilapidated chairs, a battered table, some stoves, rusted refrigerators, and other discarded items. I had never been in the place. I was not even tempted to stop and look inside.

For me, she was the only one there. I was fascinated by her, sitting in her antique rocking chair in front of the store. She appeared to be in her early twenties. She had a distinct smile and seemed to be looking out from the past.

I don't remember exactly when I first noticed her. It simply seemed as if she had always been in my life. She was dressed in a red velvet dress, very old and very elegant. Her head was slightly tilted, her eyes shaded by an antique, and also very elegant, white hat.

Some days I drove that way during my lunch hour simply to see her. Sitting in her rocking chair, her body slightly reclined and her head tilted to one side, she was the eternal spring under this morbid sun. She was always smiling at everyone with kind understanding and encouragement. I believed she had a message, a silent one, a strange and mysterious communication.

She was not shy; she smiled at everyone. At least, that was the way I felt. In the beginning, as I drove by, I could only get a glimpse of her because of the traffic. Later, I managed to slow down. If a space was available, I parked the car and watched her through the window.

There was a beautiful harmony about her, and I was afraid that if I were to get closer and stop in front of her I would disturb the balance between her and her surroundings. I even worried about the storeowner being offended if I were to approach her. I never saw anyone near her in or around the store, but I knew the owner was a bearded, chubby, old, and probably jealous man. I did not like him, but I wanted to know how he had acquired her. I was also afraid he would get rid of her someday, maybe kill her.

I surmised he put her out there every morning and kept her there all day under the brutal sun because he thought she would instill interest in the establishment. This was it! He was using her to bring in customers.

I do not know how many nights I drove home with her image in my mind, afraid I might lose it. Then I lost it.

One day I took my camera with me, having made up my mind to take her picture. I drove around the block at least five times until I found a space to park that was close enough. I took twenty shots, finishing a whole roll of film. I was so happy and excited, knowing that with the help of a photograph I could see her all the time.

When I went to pick up my pictures, I found an apology in the envelope, saying my whole roll of film had been empty. The note said there was no indication of under- or overexposure on the film. Although not a photographer, I had been using my camera for the past thirty years. It was a good camera, and this had been the first time I had gotten nothing at all from my snapshots.

I got another roll of film and went back. I used every frame on my lady, and this time I included her surroundings.

A couple of days later when I picked up the finished pictures I had a funny feeling even before I opened the envelope. My intuition had been right; everything was there except her. I was not surprised, but the meaning of this overwhelmed me. I knew now this was a secret event, meant just for me. I should not discuss it with anyone, at least not yet.

My life, except for visiting this lady at the corner, was extremely empty and boring. A middle-aged professional man, I had been married, divorced, then married again. I was sick and tired of the course of my living. Over the years, I had accumulated so many ills in my body that I had lost count of them. This event had been the beginning of the most exciting part of my life for me.

My lady with the red velvet dress was definitely not an object, but then, what was she? Driven by an inner compulsion, I knew I had to find out.

One day, after many vicious, hot days, the first hint of clouds appeared in the sky with a promise of rain that came later accompanied by lightning and thunder. I asked one of my friends if he wanted to take a ride with me, saying we would drive around and maybe stop and have a drink somewhere. Naturally, I drove by the junkyard.

Slowing down at the corner, I innocently asked, "What do you see over there?"

He surveyed the indicated scene, then turned his head back and looked at me. "Just a bunch of junk."

His answer did not surprise me.

I sat down at home one evening and tried to draw her picture with pastels. It came out looking very good. Now I had her mysterious smile, the way her head was tilted, her red velvet dress, and even her white hat. Putting my sketch in a frame, I hung it right above the mirror in my bedroom.

That night I saw her in my dreams for the first time. She was walking. She still had on the same dress and hat. I guessed the time period must have been a hundred years ago, for the streets were full of men and women wearing old-fashioned clothes. I saw myself walking beside her dressed like them. She later put her hand on my arm.

The smile on her face was the one I knew, the one that had become so familiar to me. Her lips moved for the first time, but I did not understand what she was saying. I woke up feeling great satisfaction and happiness.

The next morning I could not wait to drive by and see her. *Now she will remember me,* I thought.

She was sitting in her normal position in her rocking chair and wearing the red velvet dress. Her smile was the same, but she did not seem to remember me. I knew I must wait for another chance to communicate with her. That opportunity came a few nights later.

Again we were in the past, walking along with her hand on my arm. This time, however, a small handbag was hanging from her shoulder.

I quit work the next morning. It was getting useless anyway, having come to the point where I could think only of her. I had a burning desire to go to the storeowner and ask if I could have her, but I was afraid he would refuse. Then I might never get to see her again.

Nevertheless, I gathered all my courage one morning immediately after the store opened. I walked in, trying to be as casual as any customer or browser. The place was much cleaner inside than it was outside. There were a few pieces of old furniture, some broken lamps, more old-fashioned costumes, chests, and old phonographs.

The owner looked at me once, and I could tell he knew what was on my mind. He turned his back and pretended to be busy with something. I thought he was certainly an old, ugly, very nervous man.

After making a few attempts at attracting his attention and even coughing, I said, "Excuse me."

When he turned and looked at me, I could sense his uneasiness.

"What do you want?" he asked me impatiently.

Turning toward the outside door, I pointed and said, "Her."

He became angry. His voice was sharp and definite. "She is not for sale."

I knew I could not change his mind with money or anything else. I did not want to make him mad because I was afraid he would take her away somewhere. Pretending indifference, I asked about a few other things, but he did not want my business.

When I walked out, I slowed down. I looked at her again very carefully as I went past. She was the one in my dream, but with a small handbag. She was so still, so quiet, that others might call her a mannequin. All this time I felt the sinister eyes of the shop owner following me.

I walked the streets all day long, through the parks, everywhere. I was very restless, unable to concentrate. I did not feel like eating, nor did I want to do anything else. I could hardly wait until evening so I could sleep. When I returned home, I stared at my sketch for a long time, then I fell asleep.

I awoke with a headache the next morning. I could not remember having a dream. As one waiting for a daily telephone call that does not arrive, I had become so used to these dreams that I felt cheated.

She was absent from my dreams for the following six nights. I was totally disappointed, unhappy, and getting rather panicky.

She was still there on that corner. I had driven by a number of times with several of my friends, most of whom did not see her. One of them, however, told me he saw a doll, a lady doll, on the porch.

"This is it," I said aloud to myself. "This is a lady doll."

Children talk with their baby dolls and seemed unconcerned that they don't get an answer. I was living a late childhood fantasy, assuming all kinds of things from a lady doll. Then I forced myself not to go near that corner anymore.

Suddenly she again came to me in my sleep. This time I remembered all of our conversation. She still had that smile, rather sad, or perhaps angry. It was a very vivid dream.

"I'm tired," I said.

"So am I."

Her voice had the musical harmony of the past. I asked her name.

"I'll tell you someday."

This time we were not walking. We were inside the store. I was afraid the man would show up.

"Don't worry about him," she said. "He is too old."

I asked her how she had found me. She laughed. "You were looking for me."

I don't remember how, but she disappeared. I woke up, and her picture was not there. It had fallen from the wall. By this time, I realized I had gone as far as I could go, to the boundary of my sanity. One step further and I was afraid I might not be able to come back.

I tried to find someone to help me, aware that if I looked for support from the wrong sources I might get into real trouble. I might get locked up in a hospital and be forced to take all kinds of unnecessary medication. The mere thought of going to a doctor frightened me.

I decided to discuss this with a friend. Everyone needs a friend, but usually only the lucky people have one.

My friend, the one who could at least differentiate the doll lady from the junk, decided we should go up and see a man in the mountains. The person we were going to visit was his uncle.

He had told me he had an uncle who was a hermit. I had never seen a hermit before; nor had I ever been interested in doing so. Now, after his description, I thought his uncle might be the one to help me. Even if he could not help, what harm could a hermit do?

We drove through the high desert. It was late fall, but the weather was still as hot as hell. Bright sunshine penetrated the windshield and roof of the car. The air conditioning blasted away.

For the last half hour on the highway, we had seen no living thing. In such desolation, I could not help but feel a dread that something might happen to the car.

My friend was silent most of the time, and I did not feel like talking either. Once I asked, "How did your uncle become a hermit?"

"Just wait and ask him," my friend said.

"How often do you visit him?"

"Every week."

I had not realized his fondness for his uncle was so intense.

"I am his only link to the rest of the world," he said. "I take him his necessary supplies. Otherwise, he is self-sufficient."

"How long has he been a hermit?"

"For the past sixty years, but I've only known him for ten."

We continued in silence. Scattered clumps of brush with a touch of dark green here and there spotted the otherwise completely empty wasteland of the desert. We passed an old mining town, a ghost town now, where the only open business was the Silver Moon Saloon. Two forlorn trailers sat nearby. The remainder of the mine and the town were all well-preserved ruins. Nothing ever rotted under the hot desert sun. It simply became baked.

After a lengthy and monotonous drive, we turned onto a smaller highway and started climbing a road of winding hairpin turns up the mountain. The scenery started changing. The bushy plants turned into Joshua trees that got taller and thicker as we neared the summit. It was still hot up there, but we could feel the distant coolness of green plants.

Not too long after crossing this high mountain pass we started seeing pine trees, and the environment once more changed to a beautiful green mountain peak, with all the small breezes to go with it.

This sudden change from desert to forest was a most welcome one. We went down a big canyon for about half an hour until a blue lake appeared like a big butterfly that had landed between those majestic mountains. I wanted to stop awhile because it was so beautiful, but my friend insisted we keep driving.

"This is nothing," he said. "You'll have to see the view from the top of the mountain."

We drove a short while around the lake and then started climbing again. By then it had become mid afternoon. The trees were getting bigger and taller. My eardrums were popping from the altitude. Some of the surrounding summits were nothing but huge rocks. Even there, trees and other forms of green managed to prosper. We were close to the clouds in some places. The air was thin and fresh and cool. I noticed I had completely forgotten the lady with the red velvet dress. Nature had simply overwhelmed me.

When the sun was about to set in the thick forest, my friend pointed out a small log cabin in the distance. It was well hidden among the trees, rocks, and plants. If he had not pointed it out, I would not have seen it. Now we were on a wide path leading to the cabin.

When we arrived and I got out of the car, there was absolutely nothing but silence. All we could hear were a few birds and the sound of running water from a distant creek. It was getting dark.

My friend knocked on the door. It opened, and he stepped in. I followed him.

It was a small log cabin. We passed through the entrance, which was full of cans—empty, full, small, large—and some tools. I noticed the two cats first. They were big, bushy, and fat. One was black, the other white. They were lying down next to one another. They did not move when we walked in, but I could feel their eyes following us. A small door was on our left. We had to bend over to pass through it. We entered, and then I saw the hermit.

I was frozen, shocked. I felt that all of my body had melted. There in the corner, sitting on a rocking chair, was my shopkeeper. He did not get up.

My friend approached and hugged him. The hermit turned his head and looked at me. I felt there was something different in his eyes. He did not look as mean as he had when I had seen him in the store. I wondered if he was the same man. My friend tried to introduce me to him. We looked at one another, then without saying a word, he nodded to a small chair, and I sat down.

It was getting dark. Pretty soon I could hear the crickets through the window. I tried to ask questions the rest of the evening, but every time I said something, he answered in a way that did not seem apropos. It dawned on me later that I should have just kept quiet and listened. He was reciting something to my friend.

"Nothing has ever been created," he said. "Creation never took place. Just tell me if there is any evidence or explanation for it. The assumption of creation is the source of man's trouble. Time and place lock people into a reality that is not real."

I had some burning questions for him. When I got his attention, I asked, "Who are you? How can you be here. . . and there? Didn't I meet you at the trading post? And who is the lady with the red velvet dress?"

His answer was the same, his voice very slow and monotonous. "Do you have any evidence of creation? If you believe in it, you will never perceive things as they really are. You are a slave of your existence, of your time-space perception."

"How can you be otherwise?" I asked. "How can you be out of time-and-space perception?"

He smiled. "You are entering that perception. Just think of my lady with the red velvet dress."

It was late, and we retired for the night. I had nightmares. Everything was taking place here at the top of the mountain. There was a heavy snowstorm. I could hear the blowing wind outside. A fire was going in the fireplace. My lady in the red velvet dress was lying down on the bed, dying of a fever.

I was alone. I dashed out to try to get help but could walk only a few steps because the snow was up to my waist. The wind-driven cold cut into my face and ears. I dashed back inside. Then she died. Crying and crying, I tried to talk to her. She had that smile on her face.

I thought I should bury her outside somewhere. I remember carrying her in my arms, trying to walk. We fell down every other step. The wind was fierce. I went as far as I could go, which was not more than a few yards, then dug a grave in the snow with my hands. I laid her there, covered her with snow, then walked slowly back inside the cabin and closed the door.

When I awoke in the morning, there she was in her red velvet dress, lying on her bed. The smile was still on her face.

I was frightened. I was shocked. I thought she was alive. I kissed her and touched her, but she was frozen. I buried her again, and again I found her back on her bed the next morning. I was afraid I was losing my mind. At the same time, I was getting scared and discussed that with her. I wanted to bury her body and have it stay buried. A man must bury his dead so he can live his own life.

The last time I carried her as far as I could go. It was still cold outside, but the snow had stopped falling. I made a deeper hole and put everything I could find on top of the grave. Then I went back to the cabin and closed the door, reinforcing it with armchairs, a table, and any other heavy thing I could find. The full moon seemed frozen in place. I tried to sleep.

When I awoke, I was carrying her back into the cabin and had fallen down in front of the door. All this time, I had been the one moving her in and out, burying her in the daytime and bringing her back inside at night in my sleep.

The old man was smiling when I told him about my nightmare the next morning.

"We sleep when we think we are awake," he said, "and are dead when we think we are alive."

I wanted to stay at the cabin, but he did not want me to.

"One corpse is enough for one grave," he said. "You have to die somewhere else."

As we were driving back down the mountain, I saw a hawk circling in the sky.

When we got back to town, I knew exactly what to do. Getting one of those iron chairs from the junkyard around the trading post, I sat down next to my lady. The shopkeeper did not mind.

From nine to five, I smiled at everyone who saw me and even at those who did not. I saw their problems. I saw their illnesses and tried to help them. Sometimes I succeeded; sometimes I did not, but I was there, ready to smile and ready to give.

We talked a lot now, my lady and I. I knew her name and all about her. For many grown-ups, we were mannequins, but the little children knew better.

The rest of the time I was just like anyone else.

# Old Man

*"YOU'LL NEVER GET MY FRAGRANCE unless you die first."*

I found that piece of writing in my old books the other day. It was dated way back. It didn't mean anything to me at the time. I still don't understand much, but it reminds me of an old story.

It was years ago; I was a teenager. My father worked in a multinational company, and we were living in a country where we were total strangers to the customs and culture. Nevertheless, we lived very well because the company paid well beyond the average salary.

In a neighborhood of mostly foreigners, we had a neighbor who had a son a little older than me. This man was my friend, my idol, and my teacher. He was, strangely, a foreigner to this country because, even though his mother and father were born here, he himself had been born and educated in America. He found himself as a foreigner in his own motherland.

Our area was at the end of the city, and our backyards both extended out to the forest. Summer used to be the time of barbecues and swimming. Although our neighbors were supposed to be natives, we used to socialize with them from time to time. They spoke our language and shared some of our customs.

I don't know why I went so far in detail about this. My story starts and ends with that old man who was the father of my friend.

Summer, fall, and winter, he was always in the garden, sitting on the bench. In different clothes, he drank his wine, listened to his music through earphones, and most interestingly kept writing in books on the picnic table. Nobody in his family ever mentioned what he was writing so feverishly. Or why he was doing that. Either they didn't know or they didn't care.

I remember that late Sunday afternoon in December. Everything was dark, gray, and boring. I sat by my window watching him. The weather was cold; they even predicted snow that night. He was at the table, with a bottle of wine, some bread and cheese, his books and his earphones, alone. I said to myself, *If nothing else, I could go make this lonely man happy.*

When he saw me, he was surprised, but then happy. "Sit," he said, "please sit." He showed me a place at the table. "Son," he said, "what can I do for you?"

"Nothing," I said.

"Nothing is looking at you," he replied, "How about a piece of cheese and a sip of wine?"

I went along just to make him happy. I asked, "By the way, who are you?"

Instead of telling me about himself he said, "Allow me to read a poem I just translated:

> *"My hat, my shirt, my coat*
> *are worth nothing.*
> *Haven't you heard my name in*
> *the Universe? I am nobody*
> *I am nothing."*

"Nice to meet you, Mr. Nothing," I said. "How can I understand you?"

Then he wrote that poem on a piece of paper and gave it to me. "Besides that, son," he went on, "let me tell you something more practical: don't ever get married before the age of forty, fifty, sixty, till God knows when."

"But, it is getting cold, and they say it'll snow tonight. Please go inside."

"But inside it is much colder," he said.

I left him that evening because it was getting colder and my father called me to come home.

The next morning was Christmas day, and everything was covered in snow. My mother was happy because she didn't know we were going to have a white Christmas. I forgot the old man in the next house. We were busy picking up our gifts from under the Christmas tree when my father came and gave the sad news to my mother. They went outside, looked to the neighbor's yard, and came back in without saying anything. But we knew there was something there; we all went outside again.

There the old man, frozen like a Santa, sat at the table in front of a bottle of wine, books and headphones still on his head. I guess we were the first to give the news to his family. Soon, his wife came out crying showers. His son was very quiet, covered him in his arms, and carried him inside. Shortly thereafter, some people came and took him away with great respect, saying he was their last master.

That's all I remember about him. My friend went along his way, and I went along mine. His wife, whom I knew nothing about, disappeared. We left that country.

I grew up. Every time I was tempted to get married, I remembered him, so I postponed that decision. But I still didn't understand what he meant when he said: *"You'll never get my fragrance unless you die first."*

# One for the Road

IT WAS A SMALL HOUSE at the top of a big mountain in a small community of only a few hundred people. Getting there was a challenge. It took a good two hours to drive from the city on a crowded freeway, then a short stop at a service center where I always stopped to make a call to tell them I was on my way. The rest of the trip was a hard drive on a narrow road. On one side of the road was a sharp cliff leading off to the Rio Bravo cascading down from the Sierras into the valley. On the other side there were just the big rocks of the sharp hills.

Once you got there, though, it was well worth it.

Only two people lived in that house, but the presence of their children, grandchildren, and great-grandchildren could be felt in the memorabilia that filled the walls and floors. She was stately, like a big beautiful tree with her branches covering everybody like an umbrella. He was her husband, son, brother, friend, and her earthly attachment. They lived life their own way, loving and respecting each other.

When I arrived, the table was already set; wine bottles were opened to breathe. She was ready for grace: "We are the Sufis on a journey. We sit at the Sultan's table and eat his blessings.

"May God make this cup, this table, Eternal."

None of us were Sufis or conventional followers of any particular religion. We were admirers of Rumi, God's lover who lived in the thirteenth century, whose influence is increasingly felt around the world today. The grace was from his *Divan*.

I used to read some newly translated poems. She knew them because she was the one who was typing and editing from my horrible handwriting and broken English.

> *There are two mansions in this world.*
> *One is luck or prosperity, the other is trouble.*
> *I swear on God's name that lovers are outside of both.*
> *Death and life are both two beautiful homes for us.*
> *And many more.*

She asked me once: "I always wonder. How could anybody be so ignorant as to forget mortality and get involved so seriously in daily life?"

Her husband used to say in response, only half jokingly: "Death is for someone else. I'm special. When the time comes (if it ever does), I'll manage to avoid it. Happiness is not the destination, but the journey. Life is beautiful. I am happy here and now; if only I had a little more money . . ."

But I used to remind him, "Every party has to come to an end."

He had the answer: "Reincarnation, how about that? I believe in it. Next time I'll come as a beautiful woman, a harlot."

He used to act as though he was listening, enjoying Rumi, just to make us happy. But his love was life and anything that goes with it. I never convinced him that his joy, his sorrow, were all self-fabricated illusions. Life is nothing but a magnificent lie.

"Oh no, no, life is so beautiful," he flatly refused. "Besides, don't forget happiness is the journey. Mine is a happy one. I'm sorry for the both of you."

We always kept an empty chair for him, an empty plate, and a half-filled glass of wine at the table. He had recently passed away, and we refused to believe he was not with us anymore. He was the youngest among us, so naturally his death was the least expected. His wife and children resented the fact that God hadn't given them a warning. But I knew all the time that living this mundane life was a waste for him.

But how could I explain this to his family? They just hadn't had enough of him. He was young and nice, so why, when there are so many old, sick, and sour tyrants around, did he have to go? His family was all mad and sad because life without him was extremely lonely.

The silence that comes after death is worse than the death itself. Our rituals and prayers are nothing more than our trying to convince ourselves that we can still communicate with the deceased.

Long life may have some advantages, but it also has its curse. One sees their friends walking away, one by one. Each time a light turns off from life, the twilight gets darker and darker. It isn't the cataract in the eye, but this darkness, this loneliness, that bothers me the most.

One day I told my friends that I was going back to the country where I was born. I didn't know what really attracted me back there, but they understood. "We'll still be together. I'm still typing Rumi, right?"

"Yes, definitely," I replied.

Before I left, they sold their house and moved closer to their children in the city. That was the end of one chapter in our lives.

The small house, mountains, blue lake, my weekend trips were all in the past.

I returned to the country where I had lived as a child. The city, houses, and sea were all there, but everything else was gone. Strange savages from another planet had invaded the city.

I didn't understand them. I guess I just looked like a dinosaur in the wrong place at the wrong time to them. More than once, I thought of going back, to the place of my friends, to the land I had come from. But I didn't know if I had the time and means to do that. I remember how I felt like a stranger there too. We discussed this on the telephone and came to the conclusion that we shouldn't make any plans. As long as I translated, she kept typing, and we both enjoyed Rumi. What else could we expect from life?

Recently, I felt like writing a short story about a man who was desperately trying to dump his dead body. She liked the story. I knew about all of the health problems she was going through, but she volunteered on the phone, "Let me type it. I'll fax it to you." I waited for a while. I knew how fast she could type, but hours went by. Nothing came from the fax. Then days went by, and still nothing came.

I called. It was her husband. He said she had chest pains and had been admitted into intensive care. A day later, I called again, and it was a brain hemorrhage. He gave me the news the following day. She was gone.

After a silence, a big silence descended over our lives.

Months and months passed, and one day I was walking on a crowded street when I saw a sign with an open iron gate: Flower Passage. I remembered the place from when I had been a university student a long time ago. I used to come here to get drunk. This was a narrow street with two or three story buildings lining it (they were possibly from the Venetian period). I had never seen flowers or flower shops here. There used to be beer barrels next to the door of small, one-room restaurants. Now there were tables in their place.

It was a late afternoon, and the place was crowded. I tried to glimpse the faces through the dim lighting. They all resembled the people I used to see here before. I stopped. I felt a strange dizziness in my head. I looked inside the restaurant through an open window.

There were people sitting around tables and a big mirror on the wall, which made the place seem bigger and more crowded. I saw a raised hand in the mirror, behind the heads and shoulders. The hand was directed to me, inviting me inside.

I entered the restaurant, passing between the tables. Way in the back, next to the wall and mirror, there she was with a friend from my youth, sitting at the table waiting for me. No one was surprised. There was an open bottle of wine and four glasses at the table.

I sat next to the table. "What a surprise," I said. Then looking at their faces, I asked, "I wonder, how did both of you get here?"

"We just decided to take a cruise, to come and see you," she added. "You look so lonely."

"Yes," my young friend next to her said, "you look very lonely."

"Where is your husband?" I noticed an empty chair.

"Oh, you know him: garden, dog, life. He preferred to stay there for a while," she answered.

I felt so happy, but I was also scared. "Now," I asked, "this is not an illusion or dream or something like that, is it? Are you really with me here and now?"

They looked at each other as if they were trying to understand my question.

"Here and now," she repeated. "What do you mean by that?"

It was then that I noticed a tall thin man dressed in navy blue, wearing a skipper's hat, coming over to our table. He greeted everyone; they seemed to know each other. He introduced himself to me, "Your captain," and looked at me carefully. "You're the new passenger, right?"

Our eyes met each other. He had no pupils. His eyes were dark, deep, and strange. He carried a small package, which he put on the table. I was rather scared. She touched my hand. It was ice cold.

"Don't worry," she said softly. "All it takes is to plunge into an abyss on a starless night."

I asked the captain, "Can you give me some time to gather my belongings?"

"No need," he pointed to the small package on the table, "I brought your belongings."

I opened the package. In it was a small box. When I looked inside the box, there was a handful of ashes.

"How did you know I wanted to be cremated? Please listen, I feel like I failed, like I cheated. I tried to die before you came."

"It's all right," he said calmly, "you can try harder next time."

Then he raised his glass to toast with everyone: "One for the road."

# Kings
# and
# Crickets

As the old saying goes, "A man's home is his castle," so I then declared myself the king of my castle. I claimed further that since (according to Hobbes) the king was God's representative and God spoke through him, I would also be God's representative and receive messages from Him.

I believed this until one day while sitting in my library.

I say library but actually it was a small room packed with books stacked along the walls and cluttering the floor. I was able to put a small desk and a small bed at one corner where I studied and slept.

The rest of the house belonged to my wife, and in those rooms and corridors I felt like an unwelcome stranger. I would pass through dark hallways and see doors locked with great care, anticipating danger that could suddenly appear. When I entered my room and closed my door, all of that changed. There I was at home, in comfort and pleasure. One may think this is sad, but once you get used to this demarcation line, it isn't bad at all.

It was a late summer afternoon, and the window was open.

The air carried the scent of flowers and the songs of birds, frogs, crickets, and flies. Thanks to the screen on the window, I could enjoy nature without being molested by its bite.

I sat on my chair, turned around, and looked at the books. Some are on my "must list." Even though I don't read them all that often, I touch them every day just to feel peace. Next to those, there are others that I still struggle through. These particular books and I have been together for some time, but I still don't see everything in them. I plan to spend more time with them. Then there are the books over there, which I have read so many times. Each time I read them I understand them differently. There are the few empty shelves that wait for books I knew before but have lost long ago.

Time by time I turned toward the window to look at my small garden and the forest beyond it. Between them there is a narrow pasture where a shepherd would bring white and brown sheep, the bells around their necks sounding like Beethoven's Sixth.

But that day I preferred Mozart. There were photographs on my desk that I turned my attention toward. Regardless of their present address (be it heaven or earth), I talked with these people all the time. Looking at them gave me comfort, and along with my books I got a sense of belonging and family.

The books on my desk are the ones I'm trying to write. They have covers and titles, but most of the pages are empty. To tell the truth, I'm afraid to finish these books because I feel my mission would come to an end.

What I have portrayed up till now has been a rather strange, but happy man's story. His days belong to anybody, but when he comes home he is at peace with his books, pictures, and self.

Night came, and I opened a bottle of wine. My dinner was a loaf of bread, a cut of cheese, and some tomatoes. Naturally, Mozart was still playing. I drank for the happiness of every book and picture, and I congratulated Mozart. Later I accepted an invitation from those white, empty pages, and I started writing, but not too much. I was tired being here and now and had the urge to escape time and place. I turned the light off and went to bed.

Later that same night the screams of a cricket woke me up. I like crickets when they are far away, but this one was in my room next to my bed. I turned the light on, and the sound stopped. I turned the light off, and the cricket started chirping again.

I put on my eyeglasses and looked around carefully, under and over the bed and desk, yet I was unable to find the cricket.

"Maybe he was in my dream." I saw that it was impossible for him to get through the window screen so I turned my light off and went back to bed.

As soon as darkness and quiet set into the room, the cricket started again, clear and loud. There was no doubt this time. I had been invaded by this invisible monster with a voice like a screwdriver, penetrating my privacy with each repeated torsion.

I attacked the corner where I thought the sound was emanating from, with a mosquito swatter, a towel, and even my slipper, but where was he? To be sure about my target I turned the light off—then on—when he started chirping, and then I attacked. This time I saw him. Disproportionate to his voice, he was just a small insect hiding in an African violet pot. I threw the towel over the pot, not worrying about sacrificing my favorite flower. I covered the pot and set it on the floor. I was tense and excited with no intention to kill, but just to throw the cricket outside where he belonged.

I slowly lifted a corner of the towel, and I could see a small, black creature about the size of a honeybee. He was scared and didn't move. I grabbed him with some dirt from the pot, opened the screen, and threw him out into the garden.

I couldn't wait to celebrate my victory. Peace and dignity were restored to the room, and I smiled at the books and pictures and returned to bed. I was in such a rush to fall asleep I forgot to pray. Then I heard him again. I was shocked. How could he have slipped through my fingers?! This time his sounds were coming from behind the books. Undoubtedly, I was up against a very smart and vicious enemy. I couldn't sleep at all that night.

After my rage and anger had settled, I wanted to talk and make a deal with him. But he was as invisible, elusive, and secretive as ever. He changed location every evening. His songs had the same rhythm but different pitch and tones. His songs depended on the books he was hiding behind. Naturally he was getting wiser and smarter as the nights went on.

The cricket was included into my evening prayers. I begged God to get rid of him for me. I was ashamed that people would find out that I was scared of that monster.

Over the following days I came earlier to my room to search for the cricket. I used every trick I could think of. I asked for help from others and even bought books like *Catching a Cricket at Night* and *How to Get Along with Your Cricket*.

In the end I said to myself, "What kind of king are you? What kind of castle is this? If you can't control this one little cricket, how can you represent God on earth?"

In the meantime, in trying to exist in that little room I developed some respect for the cricket, and he did the same for me. I even thought to write about our relationship in a short story. One night I sat at my desk where he guided me for a while. I started at the beginning, and I enthusiastically brought our relations up to the minute. I was looking for a decent ending when he started screaming again. This time it was louder than ever.

"You such and such, who invited you here?! What am I going

to do with you now? I can't enjoy what I read, what I write, and even Mozart doesn't give me pleasure anymore." I cried silently. Then I cried loudly.

I knew he was listening.

I fell asleep in despair. Around three God pinched me, and I woke up. The room was still, dark, and silent. I got up and went to my desk, turned on the lamp, and what did I see?

On the left page of my open book, sitting on the desk, there was a black spot. He was sitting there quietly, motionless, and staring at me. I looked back at him. I don't know how I did it. I must have absent-mindedly shut the book on him. I knew he could have escaped if he'd wanted to. Later, I was afraid to open those pages to see what had happened. A big curtain of silence had fallen on my life.

Nevertheless, questions remained.

The cricket: Was this his mistake or suicide?

Mine: Was this an accident or murder?

But (once again according to Hobbes) there are things that even the king cannot force man to do: suicide, murder, or the confession of crime.

# Eyes

THE HOUSE WAS EXACTLY as it had been before all those things happened. After she had gone, I scrubbed the floors, cleaned the windows, and dusted off all the memories. I even changed the curtains back to beige, replacing the white ones she had put up.

It was all the way it was before, except her picture remained hanging on the wall.

Who was she?

She was an avoidable disaster before the boys were born. I once sold my soul to her for nothing; then she thought she owned me. To her, making my life miserable was the only way to love me. I should thank her. She had helped me to suffer immensely.

This house was built in a circle. Wherever I went, I ended up in the same room. A big glass window separated one room from the terrace. That was where I watched the storm. The clouds came over with a thundering that seemed to almost touch my hair. I tried to feel it, but it stayed outside.

I saw the moon and the sunrise. I saw birds. They were singing. I wanted to hear them, but they remained closed away from me.

All this time she was watching me. I knew her smile had been frozen in the past somewhere. My lack of frustration somehow amazed her. I shouldn't take life halfheartedly. I was the one desperately trying to extend her graphic existence into my life.

How did I meet the old man?

I met him gradually, silently, without introduction. I first started seeing him hanging around outside the door of my office. He was there when I left one late afternoon, and I found him still there the next morning and every day from then on.

The first thing I noticed about him were his eyes. Everything else about his body was just an accessory. He had two big, old, deep eyes. I never heard him say anything. His eyes did all the talking.

He was old, but not feeble, simply tired, lonely, and had lived many years. I knew he needed shelter, some attention, some care, and maybe a little love.

I had all of those, but how could I give them to him without her permission, her blessing? That was the question.

We walked together when we went in the house. She was there with a suspicious, unhappy look on her face. I tried to introduce him, but she had already decided what she wanted done.

"Outside," she said. "He has to live outside."

She was pointing to the terrace where no guest room existed. He understood.

"No problem. No problem," he said.

I knew he didn't want me to get upset. I gathered a few things—mattress, blanket, drink, canned foods—and carried them outside.

Night came. I tried to settle down to my routine and attempted to forget the events of the day. I knew she was also trying to forget him because she kept looking at the window. Those big eyes, like spiders attached to the glass, stared in at us. She got up and closed the drapes, but we could still see his eyes. Then she became furious and started yelling.

"Who told you to bring him to my house?"

"It's a little bit of my house, too," I said calmly, hoping to make her understand.

"We are all going to get old sometime."

"Not me," she said. "I bought your soul. You'll get old for me."

I became resigned to my sorrow. Then his eyes found me. "Self pity," they said. "What a waste. I am going to offer you your freedom."

When I woke up the next morning, there was a prayer in the air. He led me away from this place. We went to the sea. The early morning mist was all over the water and the shore. One seagull called to another. I wasn't sure if this was still part of my dream or not. I felt I had seen this sunrise and this lonely seagull before. I recognized a distant fisherman and the calm sea.

I was expecting her any second, but she did not show up. She was the only reality that had failed me constantly. Sometimes I wondered if she ever saw me.

We walked into the center of the city. Street peddlers were crowding out my memories. One called out one thing to sell, another something else. How could I be tempted to buy everything all at the same time? The constant sound around me seemed to deafen my ears.

"I'm not a music director and able to understand all this at once," I said to him. "I'm a small dot in this jungle of disharmony."

"Put a heavy bag around your head," he said.

I did and felt relieved.

We sat on the sidewalk. Traffic was running all around us. Then he grabbed my hand. We ran. We ran hard. When we stopped, I was breathless.

"Take the bag off your head," he said. "What do you see now?"

"Nothing," I said.

"Nothing out of everything?"

When we returned home, I swear I noticed that time had stopped.

"I wish," I said, "I had the knowledge of nonexistence."

There she was, looking at me from the same corner. I closed my eyes so that half of the time she couldn't see me. I needed to communicate with myself.

"It was tiring to be honest all the time," I said. "I couldn't live my life under your eyes day and night."

He went away one day exactly the way he had come. I remember it all distinctly.

She and I were sitting on the wall at the edge of the terrace, which was on top of the building. The silent city was spread out beneath us and bathed in moonlight. He hadn't been around for the past ten days. I thought she had made him go away or killed him.

"Why should I do that?" she asked.

When I asked her if she loved him, her response was vehement.

"No. He was ugly. I didn't even want to know him."

She had that mysterious smile and a touch of eternity in her eyes. Her hair was combed to the side, touching her eyebrow. She was sitting at the edge.

I don't know what happened then. Did I push her? Did she fall, or did she simply jump? It really didn't matter. What was the difference?

Her picture was still hanging there. Her eyes, her smile were still there, and the rest of me still has to live his life with two kids and the memories of an old man.

In this strange place, nobody knows where they came from.

# Birds, Bees, and Attorneys

WHEN HE CALLED, I could tell from the tone of his voice that he was in trouble. He asked me if I could go fishing with him. The inflection of his words concerned me.

"I would be glad to. How is everything, John?"

He cut me short and asked me again if I could be at the pier tomorrow.

"Say when," I said.

"Two-thirty," he said and hung up.

He was the one who had taught me to fish. He was almost my father's age. I stopped to think about age for a moment. Since I was thirty-five, he was probably well over sixty. He was a born fisherman, fiercely independent, rough but kind. I liked him very much.

In later years, I had gone into the diving business and moved to another town. He kept fishing. I heard his wife had divorced him and taken him to the cleaners because he had fooled around with a young girl. He later married the girl, and they had children. He started life all over again, but never fully recovered from the financial disaster.

The pier was empty at two-thirty in the morning. Boats were sleeping on one side. On the other side were gift shops and restaurants that had their lights dimmed, resting for a while longer before the onslaught of tourists.

He came almost a half hour late. I had not seen him in a long time, and he looked like a strange, shrunken old man in his big fisherman's jacket. Except for his smile, everything about him was different. There were large white patches on his face and hands. One of his eyebrows was completely white.

"I'm sorry," he said. "I overslept for the first time in my life."

I grabbed his hand. "John, are you all right?"

"I guess so." He smiled. "Everybody says I am."

He walked silently to his boat. I recognized it squeezed between two big fishing vessels. It was small, at least thirty years old. He knew every inch of it like his body. I felt like I was coming home.

I jumped aboard, carrying my diving equipment. He started the engine. We left the harbor in a rush. I was standing at the wheelhouse next to him.

"I concentrate on gathering sea cucumbers nowadays," he said. "They sell very well." He was looking at my diving gear. "The valuable ones around the channel islands need to be picked up by hand. That's why I need your help."

I was eager to have the opportunity to help him but worried about the air of despondency that hung about him.

"What's going on, John?" I asked hesitantly. "You seem to be very worried."

"You bet I am. I've been behind in my alimony, taxes, and other bills. If I can't quickly come up with six grand, I'm afraid they'll lock me up or take my boat." He looked rather embarrassed, even ashamed, about his situation.

"We'll do it. Everything is going to be all right," I said. I made all of the other appropriate remarks and wished I could do more than the diving for him.

I went out on the deck. There were lots of stars. The sea was calm, and we faced a pleasant breeze. I watched the white foam of the sea mix with the phosphorous from the small creatures in the water. He was inside steering the boat. Later he called me. "Why don't you sleep for a while? I'll wake you at daylight."

I knew about the narrow bunk bed next to the small sink. Before I went to sleep, I said, "Is the boat still without a bathroom?"

He didn't answer directly. He simply pointed to the ocean. "You know what to do."

When I woke up, a light was shining on the back deck. I went out to find him busy pulling in the net. He had on his yellow-and-green fishing suit. I rushed to help him. No matter how many years a person has fished, pulling in the first net of the day was always the most exciting experience.

I noticed he was a little slow but still strong and very efficient. The weights came up first, then the net. The sea cucumbers inside were like a big bunch of grapes and were sticking through every opening in the net. They were about as big as my forearm. The center of the net was filled with all kinds of jumping fish: halibut, shark, bass, and perch.

We unloaded everything one by one and put the fish in a small wooden pool filled with seawater in the center of the deck.

He stood up, looked at them, and said, "Not bad, but I need at least five more loads like that."

The rising sun had set the eastern horizon on fire with reds and oranges. A few seagulls arrived out of nowhere, followed by pelicans; then a flock of other birds started circling over the boat.

Without looking at them, he said, "They never miss. They want their share." He threw some of the fish in the ocean. A few pelicans dove immediately with their long beaks open. A couple of daring seagulls landed on the boat.

He was busy sorting the sea cucumbers but was aware of all the birds and regularly threw them their share. Nothing was wasted. The birds either caught them in the air or when they hit the sea.

We were packing the sea cucumbers into big barrels. Some of them contracted and became a small ball in my hand; others doubled in size.

"John, how big are these suckers, really?"

"As big as you think," he said without raising his head. Then he looked at my face. "Please get some of the other kind for me. They are brown and around the rocks."

"How much do they pay you?" I asked jokingly.

"That's a secret," he said and smiled. "With your help, I may be able to get out of the D.A.'s hands in a few weeks."

I looked at his face. He was serious. "Things are that bad?"

"Yeah."

I organized my diving gear.

"I'll go for a couple more drags," he said. "What a price to pay just for a piece of ass."

I dove at least four times in the next half hour. Every time I surfaced and handed him a basketful of sea cucumbers. I could see the joy and thanks in his eyes.

These sea cucumbers were slightly different from the others. They came from the bottom of the ocean around the rocks. I had seen them before but never thought they were edible or worth anything.

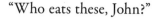

"Who eats these, John?"

"Orientals," he said. "They dry them for a long time first, then later boil them for a week to use in their meals."

"Is it good?" I was curious about the taste.

"Good for me," he said. "I have never tasted them, but one dry pound is worth a lot."

"Oh boy," I said. "Let's do it full time."

"I have no choice as long as the old lady lives." I knew he was referring to his ex-wife.

By noon he looked exhausted, and I was very tired. "Hey, John, there's no reason to kill ourselves. We'll come back tomorrow."

"I don't feel very well, but I'll try one more drag."

"Okay," I said. "I'll dive one last time."

Every time I came to the surface, I noticed the birds had multiplied. "John, it's getting pretty crazy up there." I pointed to the army of seagulls and pelicans. "Quit feeding them. Save some fish for us. We'll sell them. Besides, those birds are getting very aggressive."

He laughed. "They are nothing like attorneys, ex-wives, and bill collectors. I'll take the birds anytime."

Before I put on my diving mask, I said, "Be careful; you don't look good. Rest a little bit."

He was busy setting the net and simply shook his head. The next time I came to the surface the first thing I noticed were the birds. They were all over the boat; very few were still in the air. The others had landed on the deck.

I took my diving mask off and could hear the frenzied call of seagulls and the croaking sounds of pelicans.

I climbed into the boat. Birds filled the deck, climbing over each other trying to get to the center of the boat where I saw John lying in the pile of sea cucumbers and fish.

I yelled to him. He didn't answer me. I ran to him. Birds were in my way. Stepping over them didn't even scare them. I kicked, and a few jumped to the side. Many more landed in the space in front of me. I found a stick with a hook at the end and started hitting them as hard as I could. That hurt a few, and others flew away.

I reached John. He was lifeless, his face full of blood. The birds were all over him and eating the fish around him.

They jumped me. I had to defend myself with my arms and the stick. Yelling and screaming, I pulled John toward the cabin. I managed to get him in and shut the door. I cleaned his face with a rag. There were two holes where his eyes used to be.

I called the harbormaster on the radio. Soon, I saw the Coast Guard boat coming full speed. When they boarded, we all tried to get rid of the birds.

The Coast Guard knew John very well. One of them told me that John had had a mild heart attack not long ago. They also were aware of his problems. One said some officer was waiting on the pier to serve papers to him.

"They don't have to bother him anymore," I said. "The birds took care of him."

I packed my belongings and put a few cucumbers from my last trip at the bottom of a plastic bag.

A lady attorney and a few officers were at the pier, and they handed me a paper. They thought I was John. I asked them if they wanted a bag of very choice sea cucumbers. The lady attorney looked into the bag.

The cucumbers were melting and had jellylike juices seeping from them. She obviously did not like them.

I threw the bag into the sea. A few in the group were apparently environmentalists. One lady and a couple of the gentlemen jumped all over me.

"Why did you do that?" they yelled at me.

"I wanted to return the cucumbers to the ocean," I said.

The lady attorney reminded me, in a firm, serious voice, that according to civil code 2316, section 18A, it could cost me fifty dollars for littering the harbor with plastic trash.

# The Day
# After

WHEN HE WOKE UP, his shoes were waiting for him.

"Hurry up," they said. "It's getting late. We are going to miss the whole thing."

He rushed. The sun was not up yet. This was the time when even the most ordinary things become magical.

When he arrived at the farm, he saw they were already there. Summer was officially over.

The persons who called themselves the alchemists waited for this date each year just to gather the first harvest of the fall. They collected a drop or two of dew from selected plants and flowers at this particular organic farm.

He watched them. They all looked faintly oriental with their white hair and little white triangular beards. They picked the most precious drops with glass spoons and carefully sealed them in crystal containers. They would then dissolve their own secret material—gathered perhaps from the roots of a strange plant from the desert or the leaves of some ageless mysterious trees—into this pure morning dew. These well-kept secrets had been handed down from one old master to the new one.

Since he did not have a master or the patience to find one, he was simply observing them. He was told that in the course of eternity years meant nothing. He could not go back. He was destined to learn the secret one day, just like everybody else.

The sky behind the mountains was beginning to turn lighter, and everything gradually became ordinary again.

The ritual was finished. They all sat silently and drank a strange tea that they did not mind sharing with him.

There were many questions that bothered him. He did not understand about the space between or within matter. The difference between organic and inorganic materials, the big bang theories, and the contraction or retraction of the universe had also caused him problems of comprehension. He hoped to get some answers, so he listened closely to their conversation.

"One can participate in divine consciousness only to the extent that he is conscious of his nothingness," said one of the men.

"But we can fashion of ourselves images sufficiently powerful to deny our nothingness," said another.

*How come,* he wondered, *they talk about nothingness just like it was something?* "What is nothingness? How can one become nothing?" he asked.

"Man cannot do it," they said.

"Then what are you all doing here?" he asked.

"We are making liquid gold."

The sun eventually rose from behind the mountain. The alchemists all got in their cars and left, except one who walked slowly toward the small pond where a flock of black-and-white ducks was swimming.

He followed him but kept a respectful distance because he did not want to intrude on his privacy.

The old man was short, fat, and had a strange headband around his forehead, holding down his white hair. When he got to the pond, he called the ducks. They came swimming, flapping their wings to move faster, and quacking. They immediately surrounded him.

He was carrying a small bag of grain and bread. Once he started feeding them, the ducks jumped all over him. He stood in the middle of the noisy flock. Every so often, he would raise his hands up toward the sky. He was carrying a small net and appeared to be trying to catch a butterfly. The old man was moving swiftly from side to side as if he were trying to pick something from the air.

He could see nothing in the air, so he came closer and closer.

The old man saw him and stopped. He acted annoyed.

"I am so sorry to have interrupted you. I really didn't mean to, but I would be eternally grateful if you would tell me what you are catching in the air." When the old man turned to look at him, he noticed his eyes. They looked like distant stars.

The old man smiled. "There," he said, pointing. "Way up there is Simurgh, King of the Birds. I am trying to catch one of his feathers when they fall."

"But, sir, I see nothing but those hungry ducks," he said in total amazement.

"Oh, yes, yes," the old man replied. "You must love them and feed them."

He looked above the man's head again but could see nothing more than a branch of the willow tree, a few clouds, and an empty blue sky. Not even an ordinary bird was there. He turned to walk back, leaving the old man to his morning prayers.

On the path he saw some ant colonies. He was always fascinated by them. Even as early a riser as he was, he had never been able to catch one of these ant colonies asleep.

He had a favorite spot for watching them. He knew every one

of their circular holes. There were hundreds, maybe thousands, of these black dots carrying a straw, or other material, three or four times their size. The traffic around the opening was so beautifully managed that the ant arriving with a burden, after a few maneuvers, could get into it with complete ease. At the same time, many other ants came in and went out without touching one other.

All the ants seemed to keep busy, except for a few wandering souls on the distant perimeters doing nothing but trying to examine the surrounding area. He felt very easy and comfortable with these explorers when he found them. He was most curious to see their life underground.

"One day," he said to his shoes, "I swear I'll put myself into one of theses colonies." The shoes were silent. "Because you are close to the ground you should know them better."

"There is a little bit of the ant in every man," the shoes said, "and a lot of the man in every ant. Man or ant, it doesn't matter. When you look at either of them, they are there."

"How about Simurgh, the King of the Birds?"

"That is meaningless," said the shoes. "If you can't see or touch him, it's just mumbo jumbo."

"No, it's perception," he said slowly. "Look, for many, you are just a shoe. For me, you are someone, a friend, who talks, thinks, and feels."

He looked at his wristwatch and realized it was getting late. He had to go back home. His shoes were already going in that direction, but his feet did not want to.

He wanted to see the river, the one called Rio Bravo. The river extended all the way back into the tallest peaks of the country. Brave River was really nothing but the eternal drain of the big mountain's anger and rage. The white water rushed through the canyons with all kinds of deceptively deep side currents. The rampaging river had already claimed many lives and was looking for a new challenge all the time.

He walked upstream along the riverbank. Somehow, this river always relaxed him. His shoes were the ones that were always scared.

Soon he arrived home where his wife was waiting for him to take her and the children out. His wife did not speak to him until they were in the car and on their way. The children never spoke when their mother was upset.

"Where did you spend the night last night?" she said angrily.

"I stayed home," he said very calmly. "I slept on the couch in the living room all night. I got up very early to take a walk."

"I don't believe you," she screamed. "Go back to your mistress!"

She continued to yell and was threatening to jump out of the car and kill herself so he would be happy. The children cowered in the backseat and said nothing.

He was so upset, he pulled the car to the side of the road, stopped, and got out. "Keep the car," he said. "I will come home later." She would usually calm down after a while.

Once he was out of the car and away, he felt relieved. It was getting to be late afternoon. He kept to the highway, walking away from town.

Then he took a side road and ended up at the city dump. There was a sign that said PET ROCK CEMETERY. The smell was very significant. He walked up and down on the trash.

"How the hell do they know if a stone is dead or not?" he asked his shoes.

"You should ask the alchemists that question," the shoes replied.

When it got darker, he saw the light of some kind of fire

on the ground with two people sitting near it. He joined them. They looked rather distinguished. They were smoking a pipe, and they gave him a puff or two. It made him feel good.

One of them was fortyish with a mustache. He looked like the kind of professional that people think make a lot of money. This man confessed that he had been very wealthy at one time, but now he was barely surviving. His ex-wife had cleaned him out. She had to do it, she said, because he was sinking. She had to jump out with only a handful of money, the three kids, and alimony.

"I had to start all over again at the wrong time and in the wrong place," he said. "Nothing is worse than being old and trying to come back the second time around."

His shoes said nothing, and he looked at the other man.

"Me? I loved my children, but I had severe problems with their mother. Unfortunately, you can't have one without the other. I have the butterfly complex. I have always been tempted by the different smells and colors of the flowers. As a man, you can't get away with that. Women hate to share. They trick you and trap you, but hate to share you."

"How about our mothers?" he asked.

"Mothers are another complex. They are our worst enemies because they make us respect and admire women. You can have only one mother. The rest of them are predators."

"How about love?" he asked. "You forgot love."

"How many troubles would be avoided if man were wise enough to relieve his urges by self-satisfaction," the man with the mustache said.

They all laughed.

"What do you do here, anyway?" he asked.

"It's the only place where we feel comfortable and protected," one of the men said. "Once you are dumped, nobody will steal from you."

"And by the way," the man with the mustache said, "we are also looking for that famous lamp that has a genie in it."

When he got back home it was very late and everybody was asleep.

When he awoke the next day, it was about noon. He was surprised. This was the first time he had ever slept that late.

He was lying on the couch with an old blanket and pillow. It seemed like nobody was at home. There was no sound in the air, and he thought his ears might be plugged.

He looked for his shoes but could not find them. That made him feel strange and alarmed. He looked all over, but they were gone. He hesitantly put on another pair but felt like he was barefooted because these were not the friendly shoes with which he could communicate.

When he left the house, he was amazed to see there were no colors. Everything was black and white.

The mailbox signs with everyone's names and numbers had all been taken down and broken, but at least they were there on the ground. He looked for his name but couldn't find it.

He had the feeling today was different and heading toward strange events.

The sun was up, so he went to the river. It was where it was supposed to be and flowing with all its might. He followed the same path he had walked over every single day. He went through the same old ivy bushes that covered the trees with trumpet-like flowers.

He soon came to the small bay where the river really calmed down, away from the strong current.

There was a body in the bay. It was dressed like him, it looked like him, but the face had not been shaved.

He immediately recognized his shoes. The shoes were wet and wornout. He tried to talk with them, but they would not answer.

The body floated around the little bay, made a half circle, and then the river washed it away. The last he saw was the head, torso, and the shoes carried away on the current through the white water.

He was breathless and wanted to pinch himself but was afraid to. He started running away from the river.

Then he vaguely remembered the dream he had had last night. In the dream his ex-wife called and told him his daughter was seriously ill and wanted to see him. It was cold and late at night. Under the silvery light of a frozen moon, he carried his shoes and his long shadow.

His shoes were unhappy. They tried to change his mind, to remind him of the many times she had tried to burn him, but he kept walking.

"Is it possible," he asked, "for you to go one way and me to go another?"

"Maybe on the way back we will," they said.

He knocked at the door, and it was opened immediately. She was waiting for him and did not even say hello. He asked for his daughter. She was not around. None of the children were there.

Two men came out of the dark hallway. One was tall, the other short and chubby. One had a gun, the other a knife. When he saw them, he understood everything but it was already too late. He passed out from a heavy blow to his head.

Later he saw himself being tied up to a chair and tortured. She watched all this with a great deal of pleasure, so he tried to not let them know how much it hurt. He finally passed out and then died in the middle of the torturing.

He was still watching when she grabbed the knife from the one man, turned, and stabbed him right through his heart. No blood came.

She looked very unhappy. "You promised me that his blood would flow. Where is his blood?"

"You're too late," the man said with a smile. "He is already dead."

They took the body away and dumped it into the river.

He ran as fast as he could from the river, from himself. He kept telling himself that it was all a dream, a nightmare. Then he stopped, looked at this feet, and was terrified.

"Where are my shoes? How about the shoes? Are my shoes gone with the river?"

He started looking for familiar things in the landscape. He went purposely to those round holes where he used to watch the ants. The holes were there. The ants were gone. Newly worked ground formed small hills around the holes, but not a single ant was there.

He ran down to the pond. There were sure to be at least some ducks there. They were not there, and neither were the alchemists.

He yelled. He called the ducks, the birds, anything, anybody. He felt lonely and scared.

Then he looked at the calm surface of the pond. Nothing was there.

Nothing.

Not even his reflection.

# Mirage

I WISHED MOZART WAS PLAYING instead of this carnival music but I was afraid to turn off the radio. The silence and emptiness outside the car was overwhelming.

I was on a highway driving from one small hill to the other. There were no houses or people around. All I could see was sandy land where time and space were vibrating with the heat.

I couldn't think or remember in terms of past, present, or future. A link was broken in my chain of linear memory. My self and surroundings were totally foreign to me.

As I drove, I tried to dull the steady pain of my wisdom tooth, which had been removed some time ago, with the monotony of the landscape. I had done everything to cure this phantom pain. I knew the source of my agony was in my soul. Nothing worked. I tried religion, white man's medicines, and even black magic. This time I was going far away to dump myself in the land of nowhere.

I saw something over where the sky seemed to be falling onto the highway. A few people were standing on the road. When I got close enough, I noticed an old man dressed in a red traffic jacket holding a stop sign in one hand. His other arm was outstretched, pointing to the left side of the road. Over on the right was an umbrella. Under it was a lawn chair and a few children dressed in school uniforms.

I stopped. Once I was out of the car, I hesitated. There was no traffic or school around. The old man was smiling, his face flushed with heat. He was wearing sunglasses and a hat. I noticed a whistle between his lips.

"I beg your pardon, sir. Is there a town or maybe a service station around?" I asked.

He didn't answer. His face was serene. I felt he was looking beyond me. I thought he was blind, perhaps even deaf, and asked no more.

I went in the direction he was pointing. There wasn't even an unpaved road. It was very difficult to drive. I had to get out and push the car out of the sand. I was so glad when the car finally stopped permanently.

It was late afternoon. The sun was setting. I walked for hours. Night soon fell and covered everything. I lay down and went to sleep watching the stars.

When I woke up, morning was still a suggestion on the horizon. It was rather cold. I felt somebody watching me. I looked around carefully, but couldn't see anything.

Then I discovered a small black beetle with white shoes and a white umbrella watching me. I smiled.

He gently smiled back at me, turned around, and started walking a straight line on the sand. He came to a small green rock, left his umbrella under it, and carefully climbed the rock.

I had heard how these desert beetles gathered small drops of morning dew on their back, drank these, and got by all day under the hot sun. I was very excited to get to watch this magic show.

He stood at the top of the rock without moving. His eyes were fixed on the horizon. A few drops of morning dew were accumulating on his hunched back. I felt he was tense and thought I saw signs of fear on his face.

He slightly straightened his back and let the drops flow from his neck to his mouth. He got one and missed the rest of them.

"What happened?" I asked.

He shook his head. "I don't know. Everything seems different this morning. See, I had this dream last night. I saw the Almighty." He stopped, looked at me carefully, apparently to assess my reaction.

I was impressed. "How was He?"

"I couldn't tell you," the beetle said. "No words could describe Him."

"Was he beetle or human?"

"Nothing like that," he said. "Absolutely nothing."

He invited me to join him at sunset at the cliff's edge. "What do you mean?" I asked. "Is there a canyon around?"

"More than that," he said. "An abyss."

I had heard people talking about God all their lives. Those people were big, smart, and beautiful, but I didn't think they knew anything about God. I thought this small black beetle would talk like they had.

"If you wish, you could come with me," he said calmly. "I'm sure it's all right." We walked and walked. His white umbrella was getting heavier, but he certainly appreciated the shade. His white shoes were not spotless anymore.

"By the way," he said, "what brought you here?"

"My pain. My phantom pain." I started to explain, but he cut me off.

"Don't bother," he said. "The cure for pain actually comes from your pain. Don't you see?"

"Nonsense," I said. "I hate my pain."

✥

We met a few lizards, then a few rats. They came close to sniff us. The beetle kindly extended an invitation to them, too. They didn't even hear. The one who did hear didn't understand. The one who understood simply laughed. A lonely lion got angry and said, "So what? I am a God."

I was tired, sunburned, and hungry. I said, "Look there are no mountains, no canyon, and no abyss. There is nothing around. I think you just got me lost."

"Yes," he said. "We are lost."

"So that invitation was not a blessing after all. It looks like a big curse to me. Look around. Everybody, everything is at peace. They don't even exist by themselves. You and I, you miserable beetle, you and I are the only ones who exist. It is very painful to be alone and looking for the Almighty."

"We can't go back," he said. "We're stuck here."

The sun was setting in front of us. I stopped, looked around, and said, "There's the sunset. Where is the cliff?"

The earth started shaking, and a big rumbling noise came from deep within it. It split open.

I fell down.

The air smelled like incense inside the van, sweet and heavy. A lady with one leg was talking to a man in the driver's seat.

"We can't keep him here. There's no room."

"He can join the circus," the man said.

"No," she said. "He is useless, weak, ugly, and has no talent."

I was lying on the floor. There was a small table and bed. "Please tell me where I am."

The man turned toward me. He was very old, but looked surprisingly fit.

"We found you on the desert. You were out there for some

time." Then he looked at my eyes carefully. "Do you know who you are?"

"No," I said. He did not act surprised by my answer.

"We have to find some reason or purpose for you to be with the circus. I'm a hundred-and-three-year-old clown. The world is a circus for a clown." He turned to the lady. "She is my wife and a trapeze artist, a star. She has the record for the most somersaults."

Her skin was like leather, dried and wrinkled.

"I have only one leg. The other was artificial, but I flew over everybody." She bowed gently, professionally, then said, "What do you do?"

"I don't do anything, ma'am. I'm trained for nothing. I know nothing."

"That's good. That's very good." They acted excited. "Teach us of Nothing. We would like to learn about Nothing."

"I'm sorry, I didn't mean *that* Nothing. "I'm talking about small, trivial nothings."

"I'm sure God made you good for something," he said.

"I never met Him. If I did, He never made me aware of it."

"Ask Him," she said, jumping into the conversation. "Use your hot line to God."

I felt something crawling inside my left shoe. I asked their permission to take it off. They graciously said I could. I found the black beetle when I took my shoe off. I was so happy to see him.

"Did you forget me?" he asked. "Did you forget my invitation from the Almighty?"

I was a bit embarrassed to tell them about my little friend and our strange journey, but I went ahead and introduced him anyway. They listened with great interest. The old clown looked surprised.

"But why," he asked, "do you have to go somewhere to meet the Almighty? He is everywhere."

His wife said, "Here at the circus, I always talked to Him through my hotline. He arranges all my programs. There is a horse trainer who speaks to God through his horses."

I was like a child at an amusement park and anxious to see and try everything. One little girl said, "You can't be a child. Your face is too sad."

I said, "Maybe it's my age."

"No. No. You have never been a child. You were born old."

The old people didn't want me. They thought I was an agitator, a sleepwalker, or not old enough. That left the beetle as my only friend among this strange crowd.

One night, after trying and losing many games, I rode the carousel—a big, shiny one. All the hand-carved, wooden horses carried me around and round with the music. The lyrics said that life was a merry-go-round, up and down.

Next to the carousel was a tent with a sign that said HOUSE OF MAGIC. I was tired and knew I was at the end of the amusement park. There were no lights and music beyond where I stood.

I turned to the beetle and said, "Now it's my turn. We tried the sunset. We tried the cliffs. Now let's try my way."

He didn't say anything but simply followed me. Once we passed the entrance to the tent, we found there were mirrors after mirrors inside. Some made me small. Some made me really big. Between mirrors there were mysterious corridors where I lost my head or gained extra eyes and ears. Sometimes I was amused. Sometimes I was terrified. I realized I was totally lost.

"Where are you?" I called out to the beetle.

I heard no answer. My question echoed and re-echoed through

the labyrinth. At the end, I couldn't see myself in the mirrors anymore.

When I awakened, it was midday. The sun was shining on the sands. I was next to my car. There was nothing around. Circus, carousel, tent, and mirrors were all gone.

I knew this was all a strange dream I'd had after I'd passed out for some known or unknown reason. I stood up, took a couple of steps, and felt something under the bottom of my left shoe. It was the beetle. A black, little beetle, smashed by accident. I cried and cried without knowing why.

I opened the car door, got in, and turned on the key. The engine and music started at the same time.

*Up and down*
*Round and round*
*The world's a circus*
*For a clown.*

As I drove away, I glanced in the rearview mirror. The only thing I saw was the reflection of a clown.

# My Brother Joe

I LOVED MY BROTHER JOE from the first time I saw him with his half-closed eyes and swollen face. I wanted to be with him constantly. I purposely stayed around during the day so Mother would ask for my help. When everyone was asleep at night, I stayed next to him. Even though I was much older than he, I saw myself in him. I tried to get into his dreams. I believe I succeeded, but I didn't know if he remembered the next day that I was the one who made his dream.

I used to be jealous of our parents. They gave the impression to Joe that he was created out of their flesh and they were responsible for him, but when he needed them the most, they left him forever and went far away.

Joe then realized it would be just him and me. We had to live together. I had his body; he had my soul. We might as well get along, even though we had differences. He wanted to buy a house.

"Houses are our liabilities," I said, "just like our bodies. Besides, if there is a big earthquake, it would level everything to the ground, so why bother?"

He wasn't sure about my reasoning.

He had fallen in love every spring and was left in the cold every fall.

I tried to explain to him that it wasn't the girl he was in love with, but himself. Again, he didn't believe me and argued about the warmth of a woman and the feeling he got from them.

"It's like a sneeze or a hiccup," I said. "Nothing is left once it's over."

He was too involved with this woman to listen to me. She had such power over him that she totally engulfed him and later cannibalized him.

After some time with her, Joe came back. He tried to put together whatever was left, which wasn't much, and pick up where we had left off.

He was bald, fat, and there were bags under his eyes, but I loved him. He was still my little brother Joe.

We used to take long walks on Sunday mornings. He found his old friend, a little black beetle with white shoes and umbrella, crossing the dusty road. He asked him about his journey to the Almighty.

I said, "Oh, Joe, the Almighty is you and me and this little beetle and everyone else."

"And Beyond?" he asked.

"Yes, Joe," I said, "and Beyond." I saw signs of frustration and disappointment in his blue eyes.

"What's Beyond?" he asked, pleading for an answer.

"We'll see one day, Joe, won't we?"

He turned his face away.

One day Joe came home with this crazy idea.

"I want to ride in a rodeo," he said calmly.

Knowing him as I did, I shouldn't have been surprised, but I was shocked. I tried to ask him what he knew about rodeos. He simply told me he'd seen one and he'd liked it. Now he wanted to ride a bull. I gave up.

He bought himself an oversized cowboy hat, boots, and a belt with a big buckle the next day. When he put them on, even he laughed, but he was deadly serious. I realized I had no choice but to help him.

We started hanging around the rodeo grounds. We drank lots of beer, shot pool with the cowboys, and listened to their endless stories about horses, cows, and bulls.

Joe learned how to steady himself on top of the bull. They taught him how to tie a rope on his hand, and when the time came, how to release it and jump free of the animal.

The big day came. We saw the bull Joe was going to ride. He was two thousand pounds of beast with mean little eyes and a funny twitch to his tail.

I was terrified. He was scared but at the same time excited. I tried one more time to get him to change his mind, but I realized it was useless.

"You stay out of this. If you're not going to enjoy it, don't even watch," he said calmly.

I wasn't going to leave my baby brother in the hands of this mad animal. "No," I cried. "I'm going to ride with you."

"Don't be silly," he said. "Whoever heard of two riders for one bull?"

Three cowboys could barely restrain the agitated animal. Another two helped to put Joe on top of the bull and tie the rope on his hand.

I was next to the gate. Just before they opened the gate, I jumped on the bull and landed right behind Joe. I grabbed him with both hands.

He was so excited he didn't even notice. He thought he was riding a horse, thoroughly enjoying himself and alone. He even was yelling, "Gitty up, gitty up!" He was holding the rope as if it were reins and dug in to the sides of the bull with his spurs.

"Joe. Joe, for God's sake, let the rope go! Let's jump down," I yelled in his ear.

The bull heard me and started really kicking up dust, but Joe was in complete ecstasy. He was experiencing real power, and the beast had become an extension of his body.

"Joe, don't be crazy. Let's cut our ties. Untie the rope. Let's get the hell out of here," I yelled again.

He didn't hear or didn't care.

I don't know how long I stayed on top of the bull, but it seemed like an eternity. I couldn't hold on to him anymore and threw myself to the ground.

I watched Joe riding the bull until he disappeared to the land from which nobody ever returned.

I ended up with a couple of broken bones and lots of bruises.

# Or Is It Real?

THIRTY YEARS AGO I was told he was born with all kinds of deformities, and his parents kept him in the house from the first day on. He became the small, dark shadow in my neighbor's window.

Since no one expected him to live, the neighborhood didn't bother to come over to see the new baby. His family had not even bothered to give him a second name. They simply called him Adam.

The mother was a healthy, young, beautiful lady. The father was a kind, fragile, old man. Everyone blamed the father for not being able to make a healthy baby.

To everyone's surprise Adam kept eating, breathing, and growing, which made his deformity more obvious.

His head was almost half the size of his body. His neck and the rest of his spine became rigid, and his arms and legs didn't grow much.

I later left the town and heard very little about him. When I returned thirty years later, I happened to see a painting on the wall while visiting a friend. I was very surprised to find out Adam was the artist. I had not expected him to be alive, let alone able to paint. I asked my friend about him. I was told the young, healthy, beautiful mother of Adam had died unexpectedly, and the father, that sickly old man, was the one who now took care of Adam.

I very much wanted to see Adam.

I knocked at the door of his home the next morning. An old man with long white hair opened the door. I assumed he was the father. I had not known him well years ago, and after all that time we were total strangers to each other.

I introduced myself. He tried to remember me, hesitated for a while, still holding the door, then asked me to come in. I wasn't sure if he remembered me or not, but he certainly made me feel comfortable.

There was a narrow hall that opened on two small rooms and a kitchen. Paintings hung on all the walls, were stacked on the floor and even on the chairs.

As I was looking for somewhere to sit, he walked toward one room. He was limping, hardly walking straight. I could hear him talking with his son. My name was mentioned. When he came back, he motioned for me to follow him into Adam's room.

Adam was sitting in a small armchair with his back to me. Without changing his position, he asked my name. His voice was soft, deep, and melodic. I walked toward him. This was the first time I met Adam. Later I visited them regularly.

He was in his midforties, had big brown eyes, and bushy eyebrows. He had let his beard grow a little bit because he said it was not practical to shave daily.

When he was up, he was able to walk, but getting up was a challenge. He had to rock himself back and forth a couple of times in order to propel himself to the upright position.

His father walked around silently, ready to help him without Adam having to ask. Their motions were in complete harmony, as if they were dancing.

We all sat around the table. Adam would be on one side with his father across from him. The mother was between them. I found this out the first time I tried to sit in that chair. They looked at me as if they couldn't understand why I didn't know that was mother's chair. Mother's dishes, silver, napkin, and crystal sat in front of that chair. I wasn't surprised to find out her invisible existence in this small apartment had all kinds of accessories. Adam and his father even carried on casual conversations with her from time to time.

Everything else in this small space was also alive. They had to get permission from the bottle before they poured the wine in the glasses. The difficulty Adam had getting his glass to his mouth wasn't his fault, but that of the wine, which didn't want to be consumed.

I was amused in the beginning but later got used to it, even liked it.

I asked once what would happen if a glass was broken. The father answered with great care.

"It wouldn't be broken. It would become many small glasses."

They didn't believe in death. When I was there at night, the rooms smelled quite a bit like beans and vegetables. There was always a small pot cooking over the stove.

After dinner, the father would pick up his violin, his head slightly tilted, his jaw lightly snuggled into the chin rest. He played for hours.

Adam would occasionally sing. His voice was soft and beautiful. They complemented each other and became one.

They didn't mind me spending this time with them. I had a feeling they were so in tune to each other that they used to forget I was there.

I watched Adam painting. In order to steady the hand with

the brush, he would hold that wrist with his other hand, then bend his whole body so he could see straight. Creating took a lot of patience and hard work, but the result was usually pleasing. He was able to sell enough of his work to supplement his father's retirement income.

They were very independent if not comfortably well off. The father did the routine shopping for groceries. I took care of any other needs that required driving. Adam seldom left home. His excuses were ordinary ones common to many people, like rheumatism pains, rather than his deformities.

One day they asked me if I could take them to the cemetery before the rainy season. I gladly agreed.

We were all on our way the next day. Adam was in the backseat with his father. A small piece of luggage was sitting between them. I was curious when I saw the father carrying this suitcase out of the home, but I didn't feel comfortable asking about it.

We entered the cemetery through a big iron gate. All the direction signs and cypress trees reminded me of a strange intersection devoid of people.

We got out of the car and walked carefully between the graves down the path as a cold autumn wind blew a few leaves from the trees.

I had to carry Adam. The father was having a hard time with the luggage. I stopped every now and then and put Adam down to catch my breath.

When we came down the hill, I couldn't believe my eyes. The spot they pointed out as the mother's grave had roses and cherry trees in full bloom.

"How?" I asked. "We are in the fall of the year, and it looks like spring here."

"God takes care of Mother," Adam said very casually.

I put Adam down a few feet from the grave, and his father joined him with the suitcase.

I got nearer to examine this bizarre phenomenon. I had to look at it very closely before I noticed that all the leaves and artificial flowers had been carefully glued to the ordinary branches.

I turned back to them. They were bent over the open suitcase. I stepped away a few feet when they started toward the grave. I watched as they covered it with a plastic shield.

The father saw me. He said a few words to Adam. Adam raised his head.

I don't know why, but I turned my back to them. I didn't want them to see me there. I felt I was one too many people.

I walked farther away.

Later in the car, we talked of everything except that plastic cover and those artificial flowers.

I knew. They simply didn't believe in death.

# Reflections

I DID NOT HAVE TO LOOK at a mirror to see myself. All I had to do was think, remember him, and the way he walked and talked. I was now doing everything the way he used to do them.

Since I was his son and had reached the age most people remembered him as being, they noticed the resemblance. I supposed this was only natural. I no longer resented our being compared to each other, as I had when I was in my early teens. I had wanted to look like myself back then, or like a movie star whom I admired. I liked my father. I simply did not want to have his appearance.

The years passed, and I traveled to a faraway place where no one knew the both of us; no one saw us together to compare us each to the other.

I returned home occasionally, every five or ten years, and was shocked by the changes each passage of time had wrought. Was this what aging was all about? Was getting fatter, slower, more sluggish the fate of everyone?

Perhaps we were also getting wiser, but I did not linger or pay enough attention to him to discover if this was true. I was so busy with the trivialities of my life that I did not get to know him well at all.

Now I was back in the same condition as I had left: barefoot and empty-handed. The circle I had made to return to my origins was wide and held my ups and downs and the vast amounts of money and time I had wasted on people I now hated. My reappearance was permanent, not simply a short visit as in years past. I now had no other place to go.

When I walked upstairs, I expected to see him at the door with his robe about his shoulders and loosely belted at the waist. I knew he had dreamed of this moment for many years. His eyes would be wet and his body shaky.

I had missed all of that. He was not there.

A couple of hours later I realized I was wearing his slippers and sitting in his armchair. I did not know who put me in the space he emptied in that house, but occupy it I did.

Sarah looked at me and talked to me as if I were my father. Sarah was old and had come to our house from nowhere as a child. She grew up with the family and took over the whole house when Mother died. She cared for my father beautifully in his last days. The concern and attention Sarah gave me was comforting at first, but then I get scared when I was alone.

I began to observe every little detail of the rooms of his house, my house. There were the hallways, the little balcony that opened out onto a small part, and the bedroom where he spent most of his time. I now occupied his bedroom, my bedroom.

There were a few pictures here and there, remnants of all those years. They brought good and bad memories, which reminded me of dreams more than realities.

I suddenly wanted all of this to stop—the memories, the dreams, the nightmares. I raised my voice to tell Sarah about my new project. It would recover all I had lost, and we could spring out of here.

"Where?" she asked.

Then I realized I was the one who was still restless and unfit for reality, not her. She accepted everything in a natural manner. She had become a part of this house and landscape, like he had. The long hours of silence did not bother her. She purposely avoided any unnecessary noise or action. She only did what she wanted to do, only spoke when she felt the need to be heard.

That was the way I had been a long time ago. That was the way we all started. Then I changed. I needed the crutch of conversation or action to exist in time. I craved new things constantly. I could not stand to be left alone. When I used to say I was bored, I was actually scared to be without someone. I could not extract myself from that vicious cycle once I had fallen into it. My anxiety had followed me like my shadow did. I also remembered all of those chemical weekends.

My new reality and challenge was being here in this moment. I found myself closely resembling him in the mirror of this reality. It was somewhat scary and uncomfortable. It gave me a sense of guilt.

Once I understood him better, I became more at ease with this new identity. Even as I saw more of him in myself, I was still in full control until I lay down on his bed, my bed. Then things began to change.

I woke up, but was still half asleep. I could hear him speaking to me.

"Except for man, to be immortal is commonplace for all creatures because they are ignorant of death."

I felt like I was him. I had a foreshadowing of my coming end after a long and hard life. This hint started as a haunting tone from a clarinet or oboe heard from a distance. It was a note that soon drowned out the rest of the music. I felt this contraction in my consciousness almost every second. I simply refused to accept this as the end of my life. I looked around for help, and my eyes drifted to the small table where my medicine bottles were.

I took a pill, and I put another one under my tongue. I wanted to call someone for help, but I couldn't raise my voice. Then I saw myself next to the bed, silently watching me, or was it him standing there so still? Who was I, me or him, or had we become inseparably fused? I no longer knew.

He raised a shaking hand. He had always had this trembling, but now it was different. I grabbed his hand. He had something clenched in his palm and I took it. He smiled faintly. I felt his breath brush my cheek. I moved closer to him, and his face began to change.

His eyes, then his mouth softened, the lines smoothed out. His hair thickened and the color came back. I watched the transformation of an elderly man into a small child, and then to an infant with blue eyes and a distinct smile.

I remembered this baby from the old picture where his father and mother were standing next to him.

"Here you are at five months old," they said the first time they showed this picture to me. I thought the man next to the baby looked like me. The baby was simply another infant.

I awoke the next morning with a small ring in my hand. It had a blue stone.

"Don't you remember?" Sarah said. "This was his ring. He lost it a long time ago. We looked everywhere but couldn't find it."

She paused and looked at me thoughtfully.

"Where did you find it?"

# The Answer

I WAS RUNNING FROM EVERYONE, especially myself, like a wounded animal. My daily life had become a series of storms with short breaks in between. While I was reasonably healthy, I didn't mind.

*The premise, the basis of all human relationships is disharmony,* I thought. *Man reaches harmony only at death.*

When I finally felt tired and sick, I simply wanted to quit running and hide somewhere.

It was late afternoon when I arrived at the harbor. A fisherman was getting ready to leave, and I asked him where he was going. He was returning to the island where he lived.

"Is it okay if you take me with you? I'd like to see your island."

He paused awhile, raised his head, and peered into my eyes. His questioning look caused me to assure him that I wasn't running from the law, just from myself.

"Okay," he said.

I boarded with my small bag in my hand.

We arrived on the island in the early evening hours. It was dark. The pier was almost empty. A few boats were sleeping in the arms of a lazy surf.

A sick-looking, hungry cat came and sat on the edge of the

pier and started twitching its tail in anticipation of our cargo.

I felt a cold breeze of loneliness from a seagull as it flew over my shoulder.

After anchoring his boat, the fisherman asked if I had a place to stay. I realized that during the three hours of the trip we had hardly exchanged five words.

"Yes," I said.

He grabbed a few boxes and jumped out of the boat. I followed him. A narrow cobblestone road led us to a ghostly little town. The few people I met on the street had their heads down and were occupied with their own loneliness.

While checking me in, the hotel clerk told me that if I wanted to eat anything, I should hurry to the restaurant across the street. He said it was about to close.

I met a sweet old lady at the counter. She asked me how hungry I was.

"Just so-so," I said.

She went to the kitchen, which was on the other side of the counter, cooked an omelet, and brought me a loaf of bread and an unmarked bottle of wine. She was also the one who checked me out and locked the door behind me.

Out on the street, I could feel the coming rain in the cool wind as dead leaves swirled around my feet.

That night in my hotel room I turned from side to side on the bed for a long time, burning with fever, as I listened to the raindrops on the window. The wind was blowing. Then the rain and wind stopped. A pale round moon peeked from behind the clouds. I felt my fever break.

I dressed and walked downstairs. The night clerk was sleeping at the dimly lighted desk. I saw it was three in the morning as I passed through the lobby and went outside.

The fresh air that touched my face was full of the smell of earth and sea. I walked slowly behind my shadow. The street was empty. The moonlight was coming from behind me, and at my left was a white wall. The houses were all asleep.

When I turned the corner, I saw the back of a man standing at the end of the street. He was holding a small bag in each hand. Around him there were twenty or thirty cats.

I hesitated. His head was bald at the back. He was dressed in a heavy gown with a rope tied around his waist. He looked like a monk. I stopped, but didn't know what to do. I was very curious, but didn't want to bother him. Finally I approached him.

He turned to me. He was a solidly built, rather tall man with a well-proportioned face. He had a half-blossomed smile on his lips. He had busy eyebrows, one of which was completely white.

"Would you like to feed the cats?" he asked, holding out bags that were full of fish.

"Glad to." I stood next to him and threw small fish to the cats.

After a while he said, "We have to save some for the others."

I noticed that he had a strange gait as we walked together to another corner. He was moving his right leg by making a half-circle around his body. It made a wooden sound every time he stepped on that side.

"I have only one leg," he said, apparently noticing my curiosity.

He seemed to know where to stop. He pulled a whistle from his pocket and put it to his lips. I couldn't hear anything, but all of a sudden cats came running from everywhere. He greeted them, speaking individually to some and sometimes talking to them collectively. He asked one yellow cat about her belly. She was going to be a mother soon. He asked a gray tomcat about his sore ear.

"What kind of whistle is that? I didn't hear anything, but it's obvious the cats did."

He looked at me, then handed me the whistle. "Keep it," he said. "You should try it sometime."

I was dying to ask all kinds of questions, but he answered them before the words reached my lips.

"You want to know why I feed the cats and not the people? People are your heaven and your hell. I prefer cats."

"Do you live on this island?"

"No. I'm from another island."

He pointed to the horizon, but I didn't see anything. "I didn't know there was an island there," I said.

"Yes, there is."

"Can you take me there? I want to see your place."

We were slowly walking toward the shore. He stopped and turned to me. His face was very pale in the moonlight.

"You really want to go with me?"

"Yes."

He smiled. "Maybe tomorrow. It's late now." He pointed to a small dark shadow on the shore. "There is my boat."

We approached the small rowboat on the sand. I felt sad, afraid. "You aren't going to leave me like this, are you? I'm very lonely."

"We are all condemned to be lonely," he said.

I was burning with questions, but I didn't know where to start. He stepped into his boat, organized a few things, then asked me to give him a hand to push the boat off the shore.

"You are coming back, aren't you?" He said yes, but his face didn't have that smile. "When are you coming back? Tomorrow?" I could not keep from begging him to return.

"Maybe," he said.

"I'll wait for you at the same place," I shouted as he started rowing away.

I heard a faint assent, and I ran toward him until the water came up to my knees. I wanted to touch him.

He understood, stopped, and reached out to me. His touch was like ice. Then he gradually pulled away from me.

There, up to my knees in the sea, I watched him as he slowly disappeared, leaving a silver line behind him under the full moon.

I returned to the hotel. The night clerk was still sleeping at his desk. I climbed the stairs to my room and slept until late afternoon.

When I awoke, I felt total happiness. My body was completely rejuvenated, and my heart was full of joy. Remembering the night before, I could hardly wait until dark to meet him again. Then I realized I hadn't asked his name. *How come I didn't ask his name?* Then I realized it didn't make any difference.

I went downstairs and told the hotel receptionist I would like to stay longer. They didn't mind. There were plenty of empty rooms now that the season was over.

The weather was very nice. There were lights on in a few shops and restaurants in contrast to the previous night. I felt a joy of life in the atmosphere of this somber place. I went to a small fisherman's restaurant. I was most anxious to find out about the man, but afraid to ask openly.

I became friendly with a few old fishermen, but they had no idea about my friend from the other island who arrived after midnight to feed the street cats.

They looked at me rather strangely as if my mind were not right. I told them that I myself had thrown some fish to the cats. They became furious.

"How come you are throwing fish to cats when there are people among us who are hungry?"

One of them asked me where I found all the fish.

"He gave them to me."

They laughed and said, "Sure."

I went back to my room, lay down with my eyes open, and waited until midnight. I was thinking of all kinds of questions I wanted to ask him while the time slowly passed.

About three in the morning, I walked out of the hotel the way I had the day before. The same clerk was sleeping at his desk.

I was anxious in a way, but knowing he would be there I didn't rush.

He wasn't there. Neither were the cats. I looked at my watch. It was time, and the same moon was shining.

I waited, thinking and hoping that he had simply been delayed for some reason and would show up any minute.

I waited for a whole hour. Then I sat down and cried. I was terribly disappointed, even mad. Then I started searching for him through the narrow, winding streets of the town. I ended up at the shore, tired and frustrated.

His boat was not there. I looked at the vacant horizon. I walked back to the town, empty, angry. I saw a few cats digging in garbage cans, which they would tip over, spilling the debris into the street.

I was so mad I grabbed a large stone and threw it at them.

I heard a man yell from behind the garbage cans. I was afraid at first because I thought I had hurt him. I ran toward him. He was an old man lying on the ground on his left side. He was covered with newspapers. When he saw me, he turned onto his other side.

"I'm terribly sorry. I didn't see you. Did I hurt you?"

He shook his head. "What the hell are you doing here this late?"

I told him everything. He seemed to be listening to my story, but I wasn't sure because his eyes were closed.

After I finished, he got up, shook off the paper, and started walking away.

"Wait a minute. You didn't tell me anything. Where are you going?"

He stopped, turned back, and said, "Did this man have only one leg?"

"Yes, the other one was wooden."

"Did he wear a heavy gown with a big rope around it tied at the waistline?"

I was excited. "Yes. Yes."

He pointed to his lips. "Whistle?"

"Yes. Yes. That's him!"

"He has been dead for a long time now. He was a hermit who lived on a small island over there." He pointed to the horizon.

"No," I said, shocked. "No. It's impossible. I met him last night. He even gave me the whistle."

The old man wasn't looking at me, but he had a funny smile on his face that reminded me of something.

"It is not the answer you want to know. It is the question you need to ask," he murmured.

I noticed he walked with a funny gait as he turned and started away. He was an old madman, and I didn't think it would do me any good to follow him.

I was out after midnight the following night. The streets were empty, and a slow but steady rain was coming down. I was completely soaked as I walked along, carrying a bag full of leftover meat and liver gathered from the butcher. I stopped in the same place I had first met him.

I put his whistle to my lips and blew. I heard no sound, but the cats came from everywhere. I was happy but not surprised. I fed them and talked to them. Then I moved to another corner.

I did the same thing night after night. He never returned. I did not find out any answer about him, but I don't have any questions left either.

# The Arcade

WHEN THEY ASKED if the boy next to me was my grandson, I laughed with a heart full of happiness. "No, no. He's my son."

I watched their faces closely, simply to observe their surprise and envy. I was sixty-five, short and chunky, almost bald with a round face. My eyes were always anxious looking and full of worry; my mouth was forever ready to smile and give a compliment.

The boy resembled me a lot. He had brown curly hair and dark, honey-colored eyes. He was smart, very talkative, and outgoing. The only person we never talked to anyone about was his mother. She was a well-kept secret between us. She was an avoidable disaster until the boy was born.

I had been wealthy and successful. She never let me forget that I no longer had money. I thought it must be hell to see the world through her eyes. I eventually came to the conclusion there was nothing I could do to change her. It was too late to get out because I knew very well the little boy was the one who would suffer.

I simply accepted her as my punishment, but at least I had my reward, my son. At the beginning or in the middle of an argument with her, I would tell her I was sorry, but didn't feel like fighting and had work to do on the computer. I would sit in front of that small screen, close my ears, and concentrate on the keyboard. This was my refuge, my escape from reality.

This went on for almost five years with few moments of peace.

I lived with four seasons of hell. I thought if I tolerated her torture, it would cleanse me somehow. After all, the name of the game was mortification, the stripping off of all human layers.

The little boy was growing up in this environment. He loved us both and instinctively realized he needed us both. He sensed that loving and fighting were about the same in our lives. He had no objection to the former, but when she started yelling and cursing and I would try to respond, the little boy would yell and scream above our voices. He had a sharp, piercing tone that never failed to get attention and results. It was then that I would quit and run out of the house, very often in my bare feet. My son would follow me.

We both knew there was a pair of shoes in the trunk of the car. I started stocking shirts and pants for my son for that kind of emergency exit. Later, I added my own socks and shirts.

As the marriage deteriorated, I became more withdrawn. I spent all my free time with my son and my computer. I slept with my son, showered with him, took him to school, and picked him up after work. We were regulars at the toy section of the drugstore. I played with him each evening until he fell asleep.

The school was close to my office. I could hardly wait for afternoon when I would gather together my papers and leave the office. My son and I had full control of our lives for the next few hours then, and we wanted to make the very best of them.

Those happy periods always started under the big tree at the schoolyard. While waiting for the last recess bell to ring, I used to pretend to read a book or magazine. The children, custodian, and teachers would accept me better that way, I thought. I actually surreptitiously watched and enjoyed everything at the elementary school. When the doors of the classroom eventually opened, the children would dash out to play in the schoolyard for that one last chance to kick the ball, swing on the swings, and chase each other. I would keep searching for my son among them with rising excitement.

When I didn't find him and the last students were about to leave the schoolyard, a touch of panic would hit my heart. I would knock worriedly on doors and ask the school officers or custodians for help. I was usually told my son must be in the science or computer room.

When I would find him in front of the computer, the boy would tell me he had forgotten the time. The teacher would say apologetically that he was so good with the computers that they let him finish, even though they knew they were twenty minutes late. I knew he was good on the computers. He discovered them at home and at the arcades before he even learned to read.

I would forget everything when he would run to me with wide eyes, hug me, and tell me all about his day. Then there would be a little while of listening to Mozart together in the car, and stopping to have hamburgers and French fries before arriving at our ultimate destination: Jerry's Arcade.

It really didn't make any difference what the weather was like outside. It could be cool and rainy in the late fall or winter, or it could be blazing hot in summer, but it was always the same inside the arcade.

The lights were dimmed to almost dark. There was a smell of yeast in the air, and all kinds of smooth and barbaric sounds came flashing out of the games so that we could hardly hear the background music.

Games lined the walls and formed two rows down the center, leaving dark aisles with lines of flashing lights at the floor. Summer and winter, a couple of ceiling fans slowly turned above the machines.

Besides the strange voices and music coming from the games, there were very few human noises. Everyone, mostly children and young adults, was engrossed in the games and would rarely talk with one other.

This cool, dark atmosphere and savage music calmed and fascinated me. I was always ready to get into all these wonderful worlds of fantasy. All I had to do was place a tall stool next to my son and drop a token in the machine. Very soon we became Ninja or Robocop or one of the Mario Brothers. We could go further in stages, gain more treasure, more weapons, or die suddenly. I wasn't half as good as my son, so often I would sit and watch him rather than play myself.

When my eyes got tired, I walked around. I knew all the regulars and the manager. Though they never talked with anybody much, I had the feeling they also knew me. The manager was a dark, middle-aged man with heavy circles around his eyes. I thought the man was probably from India. I meant to ask him every time I got change.

The most unusual regular was the old man who seemed most like me, but much older and fatter. He walked around hesitantly dragging his feet on the ground. He used to sit at one particular game. He played it constantly and with great skill.

Every morning when I drove my son to school, we would pass the arcade, which was closed at that hour. The same man was always standing in front of the door, leaning against the wall. He had a cigarette casually hanging from his lips and stood watching the traffic and drinking his coffee. He would then spit about two feet away. His neck and shoulders would involuntarily tremble violently every so often. He was part of the cityscape and seemed to have a smile for everyone.

People who knew very little about his background made up

stories about him. When the convenience store next door to the arcade changed hands, the new owner didn't like him standing at the corner of his lot. He thought the man might scare the children away or at least be a nuisance. The new owner tried to get rid of him, but a few old ladies knew him and called the local newspaper.

The editor simply told the new owner it would be bad publicity for him if a brief news story came out about an old man who was unwanted simply for standing on a corner. The owner changed his mind very quickly. He started supplying the old man with his morning cup of coffee.

One of the games the boy liked most was about the birds. When a token was put into the video machine, the screen filled with birds starting their journey. The narration explained that all the birds were looking for Semurg, King of the Birds, and whoever was part of Semurg would be the one to find him. The challenge was to identify the bird who was part of Semurg.

The journey started from the beautiful, green, peaceful town where everyone was happy, except the birds. They were restless, anxious to start the long and dangerous journey. They knew only a few out of their millions would make it, but they accepted that dying on the way, even if they didn't reach Semurg, was better than staying in the village. They were like a herd of horses that could hardly wait for the signal to start the race, or like the whales who jumped ashore, believing that if they died on land they would be human in their next life.

The game had many stages of challenge, and survival was the goal. The first stage was picking a bird and flying with it around the peaks of rocky mountains and fighting with fierce eagles and hawks. If the challenger survived that, the next stage was to fly over the oceans where he had to struggle with all kinds of sea monsters, dragons, and storms.

The boy went as far as any adult in that game, but he wasn't happy. He knew he would be killed somewhere on the journey because he had chosen the wrong bird and would have to start all over again. I would sit on my stool watching and enjoying him.

Life was rather sad and somber outside the arcade. There were always unexpected troubles at home, school, and work, which were, at the very best, dull and routine. I kept telling the boy that one of these days he would make it. This hope kept us going day and night.

One day I was standing and watching my son play this game, when all of a sudden I felt terribly dizzy. I sat down on a chair. I knew I was going to pass out, so I put my head between my knees. I didn't want to ask for help; I didn't want my son to be disturbed. I thought I would be all right in a few minutes. I was sweating, could see nothing, nor hear anything for a while, but gradually everything returned to normal.

When I stood up, I was glad no one had noticed what had happened to me. I looked at my son who was in a trance, lost in the game. I decided to go to the rest room to slap some cold water on my face. That would make me feel better.

When I returned to the arcade, everything was the same except that I couldn't see my son anywhere around the game he had been playing. I thought the boy was probably at another game and looked around without finding him. I made a complete circle inside the arcade, looking for him everywhere.

I felt very strange at first, but wasn't sure what to call the emotion. Then panic took over. I started running around the video games. All the friendly machines were now strange and distant. I saw a small hole in this dark, noisy place that grew bigger every second and took over everything. I couldn't see or hear anything. My mouth was dry. I found the manager and asked if he had seen my son. The man shook his head. I made one more circle, checking inside, outside and behind every video machine, hoping to see him and tell him how awful it was for him to hide like that.

He was nowhere to be found. The empty space in my heart grew with every passing moment, and suddenly I was filled with the terrible realization that someone could have kidnapped my son.

I tried to remember the last images, the last time I had seen him. Yes, he had been in front of that game, his favorite one, busy and all by himself. I looked around again, making sure he wasn't there. I felt like screaming. I ran back to the manager.

"Look," I said, "I lost my son. Call security. Call the police."

I felt like I was on television. Two policemen showed up a few minutes after the phone call. They were very unimpressed at first, but finally they called their police station after checking everywhere. Two more officers came, and the questioning really started.

They talked only to me at first. I was grateful I had several pictures of my son. Later, the manager and everyone else at the arcade was questioned. Word of the missing child was out by then. The place was crowded with police, onlookers, reporters, and television crews.

I stood in front of them, numb and distant. I couldn't feel the pain anymore. When all the questioning was over, the police told me I could go. They said they would keep me informed of any developments.

It was then I realized that for all practical purposes the thing was over. I might never see my son again. I didn't know where to go. I felt dizzy; somebody pulled up a chair for me. I sat down, held my head with both hands, and started staring at the feet of the people who were coming, going, and standing around.

I heard my wife crying. She had gotten the news somehow. I had forgotten to call her. She ran up to me, grabbed me by the shoulder, and yelled and cursed at me.

A few people tried to console her. She seemed to be more angry with me than she was sorry for her son. She blamed me.

"You stole him from me. Now, what have you done? My God, you've killed him."

She was shaking me and spitting in my face. I managed to loosen her grip. I got up and started walking to the door. She was still trying to jump on me. They had to restrain her.

I knew everything was over with her, even with the rest of the world. I walked away from everyone and anything that tied me to reality.

I rented a small, furnished apartment. I paid no attention to my house, my wife, or my belongings. I acted as if they had never existed. I refused to talk to anyone about my son, although his picture was on television, in the paper, and even on milk cartons.

I went to work daily and performed my job like a robot— detached but with accuracy. The world around me became a dream, or maybe even a magnificent lie that was very real to others.

I wondered who made people behave the way they did. I didn't mind, but didn't understand when others took life so seriously and cried with joy or sadness, loved, hated, or even killed. I knew of no way I could change them.

Although I had lost my son, I still felt the same closeness to him, except I couldn't see and touch him. I accepted this and lived with it.

One morning I woke up with a joy and eagerness. The sun wasn't up yet, it was too early for work, so I went outside for a walk. The morning glories were still asleep; the sprinkler wafted the smell of fresh-cut grass and green junipers toward me. I wasn't sure if this was an extension of my dream or not. I watched each step; the ground seemed far away. I came to a small pond in the neighborhood park. Willows leisurely rested on the surface of the water. Ducks were all around, enjoying their morning naps. All day at work I had to remind myself of the here and now.

I was glad when my workday was over. I rushed to my car and started driving toward my son's school. I listened to the same Mozart sonata on the radio, just like we used to. At the schoolyard, I sat down under the same tree and waited for the last recess bell. I had a book on my lap, but was watching the doors. After the bell, children came out to the yard, most of them in a hurry. I knew my son wouldn't be among the early ones. I counted the children who appeared from the classroom. After twenty-eight I thought: *That's him.* He was invisible to others, but wearing the same jeans and shirt. His face was flushed and sweaty. I could see him inside of my head and simply followed him to the car.

"Where are we going now?" I asked.

"To the arcade."

The arcade was full of the familiar noisy and savage music coming from the video games. The manager was standing at his counter and immediately recognized me. An uncomfortable, wary look came to his face.

I went to the same video game my son always played. The man who waited every morning for the arcade to open was there. He still had that funny tic in his face and that involuntary motion of his shoulders. He was totally engrossed in the game. I didn't want to bother him, so I stood behind him and watched. It was the same game where the birds tried to find the king, but I didn't recognize the stage.

On the screen was a dense forest with yellow and green branches of tall trees that covered the sky and background. There was a yellow-green swamp or lake in the foreground. The man's bird was trying to fly over the lake. All kinds of flying dragons were coming out of the water with a thunderous sound and flames shooting from their mouths.

I noticed the man wasn't watching the screen; his eyes were fixed above the screen. He was concentrating on sounds. I went closer to look at his face from the side. The man didn't notice. I then moved to the machine and bent my head over the screen and looked straight at his face. The man was blind. He had no pupils. His eyes were like gray stones.

I felt a chill run down my back. I was shocked and surprised that I hadn't noticed this before. I thought that most others didn't know either and realized how well the man functioned without sight.

I touched the man on the shoulder and said, "Hi."

The man answered me like he knew who I was. The game was over. I put a token in the machine so he could continue. "Thanks," the man said softly and kept playing. He barely made it past the dragons to the other side of the lake. The machine congratulated him with a metallic voice.

"Now," it said, "your guide will take you to the palace."

A small boy appeared at the left side of the screen. It was my son: same jeans, same shirt, same round face, flushed and sweaty. I wanted to yell, to scream, to call his name.

"Don't," the man said softly and held my hand. The other hand was on the joystick. "He'll come closer."

My son approached. He looked extremely happy and waved to me. Very soon the game was over again.

I rushed to the counter, changed my money for more tokens,

and ran back. The numbers on the screen were rolling back to three, then two and zero. A sign came on that said OUT OF ORDER.

The man was standing in front of the machine. It was as if he were frozen.

"Please try again," I yelled in his ear, but the man was motionless. I shook him by the shoulder. "What is this? Is this real, or is it a game?"

"What's the difference?" the man said softly.

I wasn't sure. I grabbed the man's hand, which was moving about involuntarily. "Would you take me there?" The man was still looking at a fixed spot above the screen.

"Remember," he said, "only the one who has part of Semurg, King of the Birds, gets there."

"I want to try. It's very lonely here." I pulled the man out of the arcade. Once we were out, I realized that I really didn't know him. I thought it was a little bit late but said anyway, "Who are you?"

I discovered he was a blind astronomer who lived in the sewer and spent his time at the arcade.

"All I want is to find my son. He is all I have."

"Searching for that indispensable someone ends at absolutely no one," he said.

"Never mind," I said angrily. "I want my son. Do you know where he is?" I stood in front of the man, half-threatening him.

The man took my hand, smiled, and said, "Follow me."

I briefly wondered how I could follow a blind man, even if he was an astronomer who played video games very well.

"Do you have any other choice?" the man said as if I had asked the question aloud.

I did not.

We went into the gutters of the city. One dark labyrinth led to another. There were corpses floating in the thick liquid of the sewer. Rats, bats, and other animals were everywhere. The blind man seemed to see his way very well. I was the one who became blind in the darkness and held onto his hand for guidance. I don't know how long we traveled in that Stygian darkness until I saw a faint light that grew brighter with each step.

I found myself in a large gallery, a big arcade. Games were all along the walls, the floor, and even on the ceiling. There were children of all ages. The blind man pointed at one corner.

I saw my son. I ran toward him. The boy was busy as usual at this game. When he saw me, he smiled and tried to tell me how far he had gone with the game. I took him into my arms and held him tightly.

"I know," I said. "I know how far you went, but don't do it again."

"Why?" he asked, looking surprised. "I have been here all the time."

"Do you need tokens?" I asked.

"This arcade has no need for tokens, and the games are never out of order. Would you like to try one?" said the blind man said, who was standing behind us.

I wasn't sure. "Let me see what my son plays first." I looked at the screen. It was empty.

"How come you can play a game I don't see? What's the name of it? Who made it?"

"Do you think someone else makes the game? I do. I make mine. You have to make yours."

"Try," the blind man said. "Please try."

I approached one nobody was playing and pushed the button. I found myself in the screen. I saw a big palace door in front of me, so I walked up to it and knocked. A giant opened the door and asked harshly what I wanted. "I want to get in," I whispered.

"How dare you, a little nobody like you, wanting to get into the palace," the giant bellowed.

"But I have come a long way, gone through the gutters of humanity, lived with corpses, loved, hated, found, and lost. I have no place to go, nowhere to live. I beg of you, please let me in."

The giant opened the door. I stepped forward. The palace was made of mirrors. My reflection was in all of them. Suddenly, there were millions and millions of me.

Many years later a brief article appeared at the back of a daily paper, adding a new twist to an old mystery. While police were investigating the death of an old, blind man who lived in the city's sewers, they found a whole male skeleton next to that of a missing boy's. They were the only totally intact skeletons among thousands of scattered bones.

# The Clown

I WAS A SMALL-TOWN CLOWN with a dog and a few tricks. I wore a funny hat, a red jacket, and pants with a checkerboard design.

I traveled around the farm country in an old Chevy truck to entertain the children at small, dusty fairs where farmers brought their award-winning cows, pigs, and giant pumpkins.

I was slightly overweight and the most unlikely looking clown among all the clowns, but I liked my business. I took it very seriously.

At the beginning of my show I would announce my act with a drumbeat: "Now, ladies and gentlemen, let me welcome you to the world's greatest quarter-ring circus starring the Marvelous Sidney."

Sidney was my dog, a mixture of everything: shepherd, collie, terrier, and who knows what else.

Sidney would come into the ring and make circles around the microphone and sit in front of me on his hind legs. Then I would juggle a few things and invite a little boy or girl from the audience to help with the rest of my tricks.

At night, after everybody had left the fair, I would retire to my truck with Sidney. While Sidney was cleaning himself, I would either drink beer or scratch my back or do both.

Before I settled down to clowning, I had done a little bit of everything. I even went to college for a while, but nothing made me happier than what I was doing. I was very content until I met this little boy.

I noticed him at the fair one day. He was maybe nine or ten or even eleven or twelve. He never told me his true age or his real name. He had been coming to my show day after day, sitting at the same place in the front. He showed no signs of emotion. His eyes were fixed, and his body seemed frozen in place.

Sidney had also noticed him. After my announcement, he made his routine circles, but instead of coming to a stop in front of me, Sidney sat down in front of the boy. I whistled a few times and yelled his name, but neither Sidney nor the boy moved.

I was annoyed, but knowing that the show must go on, I continued without the dog.

When the act was over and the children and parents had left with a great deal of disappointment because of the poor performance, I approached the kid.

"What's the big idea?" I asked and kicked the dog right in the butt. The boy looked right at me. I noticed that even the white part of his eyes was blue.

"Don't you want me to help you?" he asked quietly.

"Come on," I said. "Instead of fooling around here every day, you should be in school. Where are your parents?"

"I have no parents."

He made the statement without emotion and so positively that I could ask no other questions. Sidney was still sitting there as if hypnotized.

The boy glanced down at the dog and said, "I'll have him start the show for you."

He was so sure of himself it was sickening.

He raised his hand to the dog. Sidney jumped up and started his circling. The boy told me if I would bend down a little bit he would have the dog jump over my back. To my amazement Sidney did everything that little boy wanted him to do. I knew instantly he was the master. When he asked me if he had the job, I smiled. That was a mistake.

He told me he should get ten bucks a day. I agreed.

He made more money for me in a short time than I had earned in all my life in show business. He gradually took over everything. He and Sidney were doing amazing acts no one had ever seen before. We had the best show at the fair, maybe even in the whole country.

We became popular and rich, but my clowning was lost. Later the boy tried the same thing on me that he had on Sidney.

"You should lose weight. You look more like a Santa Claus than a clown." Then he wanted to buy a new truck. "We can afford one now," he said.

Next he wanted me to change all of my wardrobe and get rid of my old hat, jacket, and baggy pants. I refused.

"Why are you doing these things to me?" I asked.

"I need to be needed."

"No, just leave me alone."

"As you wish," he said.

I could tell he was unhappy. I sat down that night right in front of him to drink my beer and scratch my back. I wanted to show him who was the boss, but it was no use. He simply smiled and took Sidney for a walk.

I knew then I had to act quickly. It was now or never. I took off immediately. I left the town silently without telling anyone.

He and Sidney became very famous and began to work in a big circus.

I remained a part-time clown in small towns, with a funny hat and a red jacket. Though I had a hard time getting a job sometimes, I understood. Who wanted to hire an aging, paunchy clown without a dog and small boy?

I acted like I was looking for a job, but I really wasn't.

Occasionally, I got hired as a scarecrow to save the cherries and berries from wild birds.

When I stood in the open field with my arms all stretched out, my head down, and the clouds touching my hair, I felt like a conductor directing a symphony of birds, insects, plants, and even people.

At night I continued to amuse myself by drinking my beer and scratching my back.

# The Stone

*The beginning of time is a darkness, radiant.*
*The end of time is a brightness, obscure.*

H. Shushud

I WAS CROSSING from one continent to another on the old, tired ferry. This old boat and many others like it, big and small, carried millions of people from one land to the other.

Through the window, the silhouettes of minarets and the domes of the old churches were like giant butterflies that had landed on the hills of this mysterious city.

The sun was setting on one side of the ferry; the other side was already shrouded in darkness. There were only a few people around, their faces barely visible in the dim light.

I noticed a small boy sitting next to his mother and grandmother. He was a spoiled, bad boy, at least that's what his mother said. He was eight and constantly demanding attention.

I found him cute. Our eyes met. He smiled. We understood each other. He was playing with everyone as he tried to pass the time. He wanted to eat, then drink. He wanted to go the bathroom, then spit. He pulled a small, colored stone from his pocket.

"Where did you get this?" his mother asked stridently.

"Your grandpa will kill you," said the grandmother in an equally harsh voice.

They tried to grab the small stone, but without success. He hid it in his clenched fist behind his back. When his mother and grandmother tried to get it again, he put it into his mouth. When they grabbed his face and tried to pry open his mouth, he swallowed.

I later heard the story. The stone had belonged to his grandfather who got it from his grandfather. Many generations had possessed that stone. How did the boy get it? He simply helped himself to it from his grandpa's old treasure chest.

We all started worrying about what would happen to the boy. He was deadly silent with a faint, funny smile on his face. I thought he was at the height of his happiness. The two ladies, along with the rest of the people on the ferry, were talking about him. Was this instant hero about to die? They didn't think so, at least not from swallowing the stone. Everyone did agree that he was a nasty, bad boy, with his grandpa's stone in his stomach.

They all forgot the incident when we arrived at the other side and everyone started gathering their belongings to disembark, ready to go to their destinations. I had nothing to collect and no place to hurry to.

While everybody was busy, the boy quietly and secretly took something from his mouth and handed it to me.

I was surprised. I wondered how come no one had found this in his mouth and why he had given it to me. But I kept quiet.

Alone, off the ferry, I looked at this now-famous stone. It was not a gem or anything valuable; it was simply a stone. I didn't understand all the fuss. I felt like throwing away the silly rock and all the rest of the nonsense connected with it.

It was late afternoon, and the streets were full of people and cars. The people were walking chest-to-chest and shoulder-to-shoulder. The fall mist soon turned into a slow, steady rain.

This was a different city on a distant continent. Everything looked strange; everything seemed familiar. When I put my hand in my pocket, I felt the stone again. I remembered the boy and the grandfathers.

The traffic signs and the neon lights with their reflections on the wet street, combined with the noise of the cars and people, had shattered time and broken it into thousands of pieces. I was no longer sure there had even been a boy on the ferry who had swallowed a stone, except that I had the stone.

I touched it again and looked at it. How indisputable was its presence? How real was its reality?

It was a bluish, quadrangular; a very old, very light, meaningless stone. I looked again and saw the million pieces of broken images on the surface of the wet streets.

I went to the old bazaar the next day. There was a spicy smell inside. One labyrinth led to another. I became totally lost. I walked into a small store and showed the shopkeeper my stone. This made the salesman very angry.

"How dare you try to sell me something? Selling is *my* job!"

An old man sitting in the shop was interested in the stone.

"This must be ten thousand years old," he said. "It came from an old mosaic. The universe is like God's mosaic made with many stones; the streets are full of them."

I knew he was joking. He didn't mean that the small stone had come from the street and not from the grandfathers of that small boy. What was the difference even if it had? I still didn't understand. It was a puzzle I couldn't solve, even though I was part of it. He smiled.

"Now you have the answer, and all you have to do is find the question. How did you find this stone?"

It was too degrading to tell the truth, so I bypassed the boy and came to grandpa's treasure chest. "I don't know how or where he obtained it."

"It doesn't really matter," the old man said. "If it was meant for you to find, then whatever you do, wherever you go, you'll find it."

Then I went on my way.

The train rushed through the mainland of Asia Minor. After a long, enthusiastic whistle, the engine stopped at a station consisting of one small, solid building. The ground was covered with snow. An adventurous, brownish dog barked from the station building. A few people left the train. A few boarded it. It started its way again with a sudden jerk, slowly steadied, then gradually achieved an unnerving rhythm.

The door opened, and a well-dressed gentleman entered my compartment. He was not young, middle-aged, or old. He was ageless. He later said his suit and shoes were at least a hundred years old.

"Would you like to know the secret of my longevity?" He opened a small box containing three olives. "That's my meal today. I chew them a long time, and then I exercise." He started moving from his face down, using every muscle in the anatomy book.

"Would you like to know how I take care of my belongings?" He religiously took off his shoes, suit, and hat. He carefully folded them and placed them in individual boxes for preservation.

I left him at the next station. It was very cold. A man dressed in a heavy fur coat met me.

"Are you a stranger?"

"Yes," I said.

"We like strangers," he said with a big smile. "You are now our guest."

We walked down narrow streets bordered by flat-roofed, mud houses. He stopped, opened the door to one of the homes, and walked into a clean room. On the floor were colorful carpets; more were hanging on the walls. There were people sitting on the floor, and a pleasant warmth came from the fireplace. They all arose, except one, an old man with a long white beard.

"God sent him to us as a guest today," said the man who had met me at the station.

"We praise God and our guest," the others chanted.

We all sat down.

"How do you do?" the bearded old man said.

I said, "If I have something, I thank God. If I don't I wait."

"That's what dogs do. Instead of that, you should worry when you have something and thank God if you don't have anything."

They all looked very simple, poor but contented.

"Show me what you have," the old man said.

I saw in his dark, deep eyes that he knew my problem. I handed him the stone. "You want to know where this came from," he said.

"Yes."

"You must go to Munzur Mountain."

"Where is it?"

"Right there." He pointed to the window through which I could see a majestic, rugged, snow-covered mountain.

I was shocked. I knew he was telling me the truth, but I wasn't sure whether I liked a mountain this size.

He smiled and said, "You could wait until next spring, next summer, next fall, or next winter."

"What's up there?" I had already waited too long.

"You'll see when you get there," he told me.

My journey to the summit of Munzur Mountain started the next day.

I wasn't trained for this journey, nor dressed for it. All I had was this unquestionable desire and killing curiosity. My guide was the man who had met me at the station.

It was a long, hard journey. I listened to the whistle of the cold wind through the rocks as it cried wolf at the darkness. Our path was guided by the sun above, and at night we tried to find the way by the stars.

It became colder and harder to climb as we got higher, but my guide had taken this journey before. He knew every step of the way. We would soon reach the point of no return. I knew this right from the beginning.

I sometimes felt lost in this great, white nowhere. I cried until I found my way through the glaciers. There were days when we ate nothing. There were nights when we didn't sleep.

Then one morning I felt I had conquered this majestic mountain. I could see the top of it.

At the top the wind was deafening. It was hard to walk, to breathe, even to stand. At the summit I saw shapely heads carved in stone. I didn't know if they had been fashioned there or carried up by some mysterious power.

They were like Absolute Beings. I was frozen not only by cold but also by excitement.

My guide led me close to one of them. Even though they were thousands of years old, they were still very strong as they looked out at the horizon with a certain pride.

My guide pointed out a small crack. There were some missing

chips in one eye. I immediately knew my stone would match this area. I carefully placed the stone in the empty space.

Suddenly I felt silence all over me and all around me. Then I saw Nothingness like a Christmas tree.

When I told this to the old man later, he wasn't impressed.

"No, you didn't see Nothing. It is not that easy. You have to take yourself out of the way first. Then you'll see the way God sees and hear the way God hears."

"How do you do that?" I asked.

"Simply," he said. "Find a job, marry a woman, suffer all the problems of everyday life, live like everyone, except when your hands are at work, your heart should be somewhere else."

# The Toy Maker

THE GRAND TOYS were all made in the old days, and there wasn't anything new or interesting anymore. I had been very lucky over the years to be able to collect the best of the old toys at very reasonable prices.

People were usually very glad to get rid of them. They thought toys belonged to children. Grown-ups didn't need them, especially to talk to them the way I did.

I had been conversing with toys all my life. Even knowing them for what they were had never bothered me. I believed they had souls like the rest of us and that, if we addressed them properly, they would converse with us.

For as long as I could remember, I woke my dolls up every morning. Some were in my bedroom, others spread all over the house. I wound them up one by one with the first light of the sun and let them go.

They jumped, walked, and ran with harmony or disharmony, depending on their mood. Some of them stopped every so often, played a few beats on their drum, then marched on. A few girl toys danced around. Some rode in cars, others on horses. Some of the toys kissed, others fought.

I stood back and enjoyed them, but it was never very long before I would get involved and find myself right in the middle of the crowd. I also sang, danced, loved, hated. I often forgot which one of us was the toy and which one was real.

In order to be able to sleep, I had to stay awake all day long, and my toys understood that. Eventually some of them slowed down and stopped. By then I was also tired and ready to rest.

In the middle of one night, when I was deep in my sleep, I was awakened by a steady drumbeat. At first I thought it was coming from outside. Then I realized something was moving on the floor and I turned on the light. It was my favorite toy, a little drummer boy, marching around as if it was daytime. The other toys were also awakened.

I was surprised, grabbed his right arm, and pushed his off button.

"You bad boy," I said. "What are you up to? Sleepers don't like marching boys in the middle of the night."

He stopped, but I started wondering who had wound him up. I knew his spring couldn't go on day and night. It was too late to worry, and I desperately wanted to go back to sleep. So did the other toys.

The first thing I did the next morning was check the drummer boy. I picked him up and examined him thoroughly. Everything seemed to be in order. Then I wound him and let him go with the others.

The same thing happened that night, the night after, and the one after that.

I tried hard to find the problem so I could fix him but was unable to come up with anything. I lost sleep.

Annoyed at first, I later became furious. I wanted to throw the drummer boy out of the window or break him to pieces with a big hammer, but I was afraid of the other toys. If they should get mad at me, they might do the same thing as the drummer boy.

I thought of moving to another house and living all by myself, but I knew it would be impossible for me to exist without my toys.

In the end, I decided I should look for a toy maker, a master who knew how to repair toys. I was told by several people who knew everything that all the famous toy makers had lived and died long ago. Handcrafted toys were a thing of the past. Since there was not much use for new ones, nobody even bothered to learn the secret of toy making. Most toys were made in factories and battery operated.

I didn't want to believe that. I looked all over town and searched the yellow pages of the telephone books. I did not find anyone who could answer my need.

My night misery went on. I was awakened at all odd hours by the drummer boy. Later on, a flute girl and others joined the rebel. They played their music and ran around all evening. I had no way of knowing which one would wake me up to face this unpleasant reality.

I was about to give up my search for the Master Toy Maker until one late afternoon. I stopped at the secondhand thrift store, the graveyard of our memories, where one can find a secondhand wife, child, or toys.

At the back of this store I found a man about my age who looked exactly like me. He was working in a small room making toys. He was busy cutting and carving wood.

"All toys are there in the wood," he said.

He was simply cutting and eliminating the unwanted parts. A new toy in a different shape and size came into existence every minute.

I watched him with great excitement. My heart almost stopped.

I knew I had found him at last. Even though he looked exactly like me, I still called him Mister.

"Mister, you must be the one I have been looking for all over. When I found you, I thought you were me, but whoever you are, you have to help me. I have this problem."

I went on to tell him all about my toys and the trouble I had been having with them recently. "Please, help me!"

He was busy cutting wood and didn't hear me. I approached him and grabbed him by his shoulders.

"Listen. Listen to me now! I have a couple of broken toys. Would you repair them for me?"

He shook his head. "I am just a toy maker. You must find a real one."

I was so angry, so disappointed, I couldn't talk or move for a while.

I went home empty-handed. I was frightened by the night. "For God's sake, does anyone know where the real toy maker is?"

When night came, I put all the toys to sleep and stayed awake. When the clock struck midnight, I grabbed the drum and marched around and around until morning, hopelessly beating my drum, trying to wake up everyone.

# Transformation

I SUDDENLY COUGHED ONE AFTERNOON, a violent, racking exhalation of air. Then blood rose to my mouth.

I understood everything at once, but it was already too late. I looked and saw life flowing all around me, naturally, beautifully. Everyone was busy doing their own living.

Then I went through the rest of it: a few tests, a few doctors, a few head shakes, and the somber, sad news came at the end.

"You have cancer in your chest. Unfortunately, it has already gone beyond the point where it can be operated on and removed."

When I first heard this, I had the feeling the doctor was talking about someone else. I looked in his eyes and became resigned to the truth. This was it for me, and I relaxed.

I was amazed to discover that dying immediately released me from millions of life's little problems. Death was a big one that overshadowed all of the others.

I was suddenly a free man, but felt the darkness of death enshroud my life at the same time. I had lived all of these years while having conveniently managed to forget the very existence of death.

Who made me forget? Who had fooled me all of this time? Now I was facing death. I realized it had always been around. It was huge, so real—as vast as the sky. How could I have missed seeing it all these years?!

Life had been nothing but a magnificent lie and a joke, but one in which everyone was seriously involved.

I had witnessed the end of a few living things, even humans, but I thought I was an exception. I would live indefinitely, and maybe sometime in the far future, while I was asleep, I would gradually fade away in some manner, but certainly not like this, not in the middle of my life with a foreign tissue growing right inside my chest like an octopus that was grabbing and suffocating every part of my body. How could I have hidden my enemy and nourished him with my own blood? How could God and science allow this?

If we were all going to die, why were we born?

This was a question for God. Then I realized I didn't know anything about God, so how could I direct this question to him?

I had to believe in my ignorance about death, life, and God. I quickly discovered that most people I asked were as unenlightened as I was.

I blamed the artists, scientists, and writers because all of their vast talents had been spread out to encompass the trivial matters of the world. How could they have considered anything else until the life-and-death issue had been settled? Who made us forget about death?

Here I was in the middle of my expected life span, and I had to say good-bye to this body I had borne and cared for and liked and grown accustomed to all these years. If by now I was used to this reality, death was another one about which I knew nothing. Death was now a tangible entity looming before me and bigger than the sky. I was scared. This body was not like shirts or socks to be thrown away when worn out. This was my body, good and bad. It was me that I had to give up.

I thought I should share my discovery with others. I wanted to warn everyone about death so they wouldn't be as surprised as I was.

I put all of my feelings in writing and took them to several publishers. I was completely ignored by most, but a few who cared enough to glance at my work were not interested.

"It's too morbid. It won't sell."

"Life is morbid," I said.

"Yes, but it's not proper nor profitable to remind people about their mortality. Who do you think you are?"

I couldn't discuss my qualifications with them. All I could say was, if I had known before what I knew now, I could have lived my life differently.

I felt that time had stopped and a dark shadow had fallen in front of me. I felt like a wounded animal on the run from his pain.

All the pleasures, challenges, even the worries were all things of the past. One big eclipse covered everything.

I had to find something that could modify my present reality.

I went through a period of soul searching, rummaging among noble and other causes. Even the most daring or foolish acts under normal circumstances meant very little because the gains or losses at the end of each action had already been forfeited.

I needed to be a martyr in the holy war against myself, not for any other concrete purpose, because I didn't have one.


I discovered the place by accident. I was walking around a shopping mall when someone opened a door and said, "Welcome."

I walked in. It was a strange place with game rooms, stages, and a big screen for showing pictures. Pizza and other fast foods were being served.

Children and adults filled the rooms and hallways. All seemed to be in a festive mood.

I sat at a table where I could see the stage. There was a band of stuffed animals dressed like people. They were seated on the stage and playing the piano, guitar, drums, and other instruments.

The lights went off. They came alive and started singing and talking.

I was speechless. I knew they were mechanically animated, but this didn't stop me from becoming involved with them. I changed tables to sit at the long one next to the stage where I could see them better. The lights went off and on. I sat there for a while.

I later got up to find something to drink, then came back to my table. When I returned, I noticed the black man at the piano. He seemed to recognize me. He nodded his head slightly in my direction and smiled.

I went to the game room. Everyone was concentrating on their plays. I found a jet plane and sat in it. I deposited a quarter, and the game started.

I thought that flying a jet and shooting at enemy planes was a complicated endeavor, happened only in wars, and a person needed rigorous training for it. When I sat down in the cockpit of the jet, I felt awkward. I was demolished by the first enemy gun, but I later became quite good. I was flying over the mountains, down the valleys, and avoiding most of the enemy fire. I did not think I had done as well as one of the previous players, but I was satisfied. The best part of playing was that I totally forgot my problem.

I moved to a space game where I was to defend Earth from creatures out of the unknown fringes of the galaxy. They were short, wore funny dresses, and were clearly bisexual. Instead of saving the earth, I got lost in space.

I continued to wonder about the stage in the other room as I played the games. I could hear the concert and decided to return.

I found some kids sitting at my original table when I went in, so I sat next to one of them.

Eight children and a few parents were celebrating the birthday of a small girl. There were six candles on her cake. Everyone in their group was wearing a funny hat, and they had many balloons. After the little girl blew out the candles, they all sang "Happy Birthday," joined by the people on the stage. The black man seemed happy and gave me his special smile. Before I realized what I was doing, I found myself singing along with them.

Birthday celebrations went on all night long, and I took part in all of them.

I got home about midnight. Although my wife said she was worried, I knew she was simply upset. She didn't believe me when I told her where I had been. She was sure I'd been out with someone else. Even at this juncture in our life, having me be with someone else was worse than seeing me dead. She had a strange theory about who was going to go first.

Life was not the place to look for a lot of sense. The only real event in life was death. Everything else was relative.

With that understanding, the major issue was not why we did not kill ourselves, but why we lived a life over which we had no control or of which we had no knowledge. The only consolation was that we could quit this life whenever we wanted to. I made it a habit to carry all of my sleeping pills with me for that reason. I had twenty of them.

Man's biggest threat was standing before God on judgment day. When the last breath was gone, it was not a body, but simply a corpse to be disposed of. Then a person arrived at God's court where the pluses and minuses of his life would be counted.

There certainly must be a better theory than that.

What a mystery! I forced myself to find out what would happen to me immediately after my death. If I had strong ties to life, it would be tough to release myself. If I were too preoccupied with the end, I would miss the chance to live my life as it was unfolding.

Once I knew the end, and I hoped I was beginning to, I could live much more intelligently. I simply needed to paint the picture according to the frame. I had been paying too much attention to life, and very little attention to death. That was wrong.

This was not worshipping death. Death was more natural and stronger than that. I was against this miscalculation and misjudgment about life. How many human values could be measured up to with the right perspective on life and death?

The idea of living as if there were forever or that death would come tomorrow was not reality.

As long as we don't know death, we also don't know life, so both of them escape our reality. All we know about life is incomplete, an imperfect perception. It was unknown, and one should not count unknowns.

*Man is the touching point of these two unknowns. Like a shore or horizon, it is not an object, but a concept.*

I accepted this as another erroneous description. As long as we stayed on this level we could not help but fail.

Was dying before my death chronologically possible? I did not know. Assuming it was, how could it be achieved?

Could a person melt away the self?

I knew some people who formed a bigger and harder self. The self was not such an easy target that it could be demolished with a touch of humiliation and sacrifice. It took much more than that. A person had to take a more serious approach.

We suffered when we went through unpleasant experiences.

This was not by choice. A person could hit his head against the walls only so many times. These experiences came with life.

My older son, who was in high school, worried about his future and mine. I could see his concern for my health was influenced by all the uncertainty and inconveniences he was anticipating after my departure.

*Departure.* That was the word the funeral director used when I wanted to arrange for his services. He was well dressed, well mannered, and a very enthusiastic salesman. He told me he was going to give me a good package deal if I bought a certain plot where all the family could be together. He showed me a picture of the cemetery with its well-trimmed lawn, rubber statue of the Last Supper, and other religious doodads.

I asked him if he had his funeral all planned, too. That obviously surprised him. I could see annoyance and anxiety in his eyes. He tried to avoid answering but said, "Well, I've never thought about it."

The insurance agent I talked to was the same way.

I wanted to stay at work as long as possible before my actual departure, but when the big news hit company headquarters I was given my pension card of appreciation and forced into an early retirement.

The night after my last day with the company I thought about the need for someplace to deal with the end of a person's life. Since we had all kinds of institutions to prepare us for our entrance into this world, we really should have some place to prepare us for our exit.

Our departure from this world seemed to be all hushed up. Even the funeral industry was capitalizing on the idea of going to heaven with class. Was seeing that the body rested in a comfortable coffin the best thing we could do for our deceased?

What about religion?

Since I had not asked anyone's consent to come here, I didn't think going away should be anybody's business but my own.

I went to a priest. My first question was, "Why me?"

He was a professional in his business. He smiled happily. I knew what he was saying to himself: *Thank God it's not me.*

"We are all going to go to God," he said in a pious manner.

"I never thought I had been away from God, Father."

"That's good. That's good." He was restless, in a hurry. "Come back sometime tomorrow." He paused. "Have you had confession lately?"

That was my last visit to him. I thought about looking for some other priest, but I was afraid I didn't have enough time. The time I had left seemed very valuable to me.

I had an appointment with a specialist the next day, a doctor who concentrated his practice on patients like me. I was curious. I wanted to see other people with a similar diagnosis as mine, but at different stages in the progression of the disease. I basically knew what was going to happen to me, but I wanted to see it with my own eyes.

The doctor's office had a rather large waiting room with oil paintings, a few plants, chairs, and comfortable lounges. The people sitting around the room were all different. I used to think most people would look the same at the end, like babies are in the beginning. I was wrong.

Some of the people were just hanging in there with faces like paper, while others looked anxious or in pain, and some were simply lost in their thoughts. None of them looked active; some looked barely alive.

I could not identify with any of them. Because of this, I think I was expecting the doctor to tell me this was a mistake, I had a minor but bad cold, and I didn't really belong here.

A receptionist gave me a form to fill out. Some of the questions were about my age and race. The rest of them were about my insurance and who would be responsible for the bill. I knew she was doing her best to find out what kind of monetary return I represented to her employer.

After I convinced the receptionist I was not a freeloader, she seemed to feel better about me. She was a very attractive girl. I liked her legs and hips. When I showed my appreciation for her femininity, she was flattered.

Then I remembered my wife. She had told me before I left home that I should be careful about nurses because of what she had seen on her two favorite soap operas. It all sounded like a gigantic bit of nonsense to me. My wife paid so much attention to such darn nonsense that it actually blinded her to my immediate future. It really made me realize that we all die alone.

I thought of a sheep standing before the butcher who wanted his meat. I wanted my life.

The doctor was another story. He could not guarantee that anything would extend my life for one hour, one week, or one month, but I felt assured his treatment would add more misery to whatever time I had left. I would have more nausea, weakness, fever, and misery added to the remainder of my existence. At best, I might have a slight chance of living for as long as a year, or at least a few months.

I thought this doctor had gained a very lucrative business from people who did not accept what was natural and who wanted to live at any expense. That represented a fortune for this man.

I refused to spend any more time than I could help in places like this with unaccepting people.

The highlight of recent days and weeks was the last total eclipse of the century. I read everything about it I could find in the local newspapers. The articles kept saying people shouldn't look at an eclipse without protection for their eyes.

How could I miss seeing the last eclipse of this century? The next one wouldn't be for many, many years. Since I was fascinated by the northern lights, I felt my body was aching for the sight of the eclipse. My frustration was the same as germinating seeds trying to penetrate the earth.

I knew I would come back to life once I had lived under the northern lights. With due respect to all worshippers of the sun or the moon, I preferred the northern lights.

All light came from the sun. The sun was a big explosion, that forbidden start. I thought the northern lights came when the sun went into a full eclipse. Instead of going to the Arctic to see the northern lights, I thought I would have them right here during the eclipse.

I left the house early in the morning, praying the sky would be clear. I climbed a small hill for the best view.

The clouds started gathering, and I thought it was going to rain. I felt so sad when it looked like my chances of seeing this eclipse of the century were getting slimmer.

At exactly 10:45 the sun started getting darker. It took only three minutes before it was completely covered by a dark shadow except for a circle of semi-bright shadow. This was my northern light. I don't care what anybody else called it. This was my northern light.

The sky was cloudy, but I could see that mysterious, beautiful light that brought tears to my eyes and heart. I was in ecstasy. I was so excited I screamed, I cried.

The sun soon started getting brighter; everything returned

to normal and became ordinary again, except my body. I felt I had accumulated all the energy from the northern lights and had flushed all the cancer cells from my chest.

I so wanted to believe in miracles, but I had no control over the following days. My health had deteriorated in the last couple of weeks. It became hard for me to walk even a short distance. My brain was the same, but not my lungs. As long as I didn't have excruciating pain, I would manage without drugs.

I spent some time and took care of my will, my bank account, and my insurance, but I was most anxious to go back to that place with all the games and the birthday parties. I was haunted by the shadow of death, so I took refuge in that strange place.

It wasn't as busy as the first time I was there. There were only a few groups of children at the tables for birthday parties. I went to the arcade where the games were, trying to figure out one of them or how best to play them. A little boy approached me.

"Hey, Mister, may I play with you?"

I immediately noticed his eyes. They were black, so dark I couldn't see the pupils at the center.

I looked around. No one seemed to be with him. He didn't even wait for my answer. He grabbed my hand and dragged me to a game made up of nails. There were all colors and sizes of nails on the screen. When he pushed the button, the nails were all moved around me into all kinds of shapes. A light source with many colors came through the screen. I saw everything I could have dreamed about.

"That's Lumiere, the game that's made me the most happy," the boy said with authority.

I looked at him again, doubting his age. "How old are you, anyway?"

"I have a birthday every day here. What do you think about this game?"

I didn't have an answer.

"It's not the event, but the perception that is the most important thing. The elements are all the same. What you would call creation is just a simple illusion. Nothing has ever changed. Right?"

"Right," I said. There was no question about it. This kid was some kind of genius, but when I got over my wonder he started bothering me.

I excused myself and walked to the stage. The band was in full action. Red and white lights were flashing in time to the rhythm being played on the organ in front of the black man. The drummer was as happy as when I left last time, and the rest of them had the same joyous expressions on their faces.

I sat next to the stage. I was physically and mentally tired. I pushed all of my worries out of my mind and tried to empty myself of all thoughts.

Then everything started to happen at once. All the animated stuffed toys became alive to me. I wanted to find that little fellow, since I felt he was the only one who could understand this and believe me.

I looked all around. Everybody was in their own world, playing their own game. Then he came to me with a smile.

"Can I sit with you?"

Without waiting for an answer, he sat next to me. He first touched, then held, my hand. He was trying to comfort me, I thought.

"This is it," he said calmly. "Everyone comes to this point sooner or later."

"I'm afraid," I said.

"Why?" His question was steel cold.

"I am afraid to let go. Life is something I have become accustomed to. It's not like taking off a dirty shirt or socks."

"But," he said, "you were at the bottom of Hell. Now you are scared of immortality." There was a touch of disappointment and impatience in his voice.

"Tell me, is there any chance to come back here again afterward?"

"Where?" he asked, looking around and giving me an odd questioning glance. "If you want to, yes, you can come back here."

I felt satisfied with his answer.

We walked through long hallways that led us to another corridor. Finally, we stopped in front of a door. I read the small sign that said STAFF ONLY.

When we went inside, I was undressed completely, and my clothes were put on a big stuffed doll that looked like me. My little friend kept reminding me about the game of Lumiere. I felt very free and happy without anything to remind me about me.

"Now your body is going to go through some changes," he said.

Suddenly I saw myself on my own bed, sleeping. I saw a woman next to me, helplessly trying to wake me up. Then she discovered the pillbox with the tablets I used to take occasionally for sleeping. It was empty. I didn't understand why she started screaming.

I had no desire to wake up.

# Apocalypse

THE ARCHANGEL BECAME MOST CONCERNED after listening to the creatures of the Universe.

They seemed very determined in annihilating themselves unless God appeared to them to answer their prayers and end His separation.

They were ready to climb Mount Sinai and jump into the abyss.

When Gabriel asked them, "Why not be content with His messengers?" They answered, "Please, no more messengers, they are confusing and dividing us."

Their fire of separation was so intense, Archangel Gabriel was afraid; it may cause the Universe to blow up in a terminal big bang.

At the throne, the Almighty listened and said, "I gave them a life to live, why not be happy with that?"

The Archangel hesitated to tell what he heard from them. "Give us one good reason to live!" was their reply.

Instead He said, "My Lord they want permanency, immortality."

"All right!" God cut him short, "Tell them to be ready." This order was too big even for the Archangel.

The moment came, and every being dressed their best.

They climbed Mount Sinai and lined up at the edge of the Abyss. They yelled and cried together. "Where are you?"

Their primordial scream reverberated in the emptiness. This came back to them:

"Where are you?"

Then every existence started disappearing in Absence, like sugar in the water.

# BOOKS OF RELATED INTEREST

### The Forbidden Rumi
The Suppressed Poems of Rumi on Love, Heresy,
and Intoxication
*Translations and Commentary by Nevit O. Ergin
and Will Johnson*

### The Rubais of Rumi
Insane with Love
*Translations and Commentary by Nevit O. Ergin
and Will Johnson*

### The Spiritual Practices of Rumi
Radical Techniques for Beholding the Divine
*by Will Johnson*

### Sufi Rapper
The Spiritual Journey of Abd al Malik
*by Abd al Malik*

### Journey to the Lord of Power
A Sufi Manual on Retreat
*by Ibn Arabi, with commentary by Abd al-Kerim al-Jili
Translated from the Arabic by Rabia Terry Harris*

### The Book of Sufi Healing
*by Shaykh Hakim and Moinuddin Chishti*

### The Way of Sufi Chivalry
*by Ibn al-Husayn al-Sulami*

### Muhammad
His Life Based on the Earliest Sources
*by Martin Lings*

INNER TRADITIONS • BEAR & COMPANY
P.O. Box 388 • Rochester, VT 05767
1-800-246-8648
www.InnerTraditions.com
Or contact your local bookseller